KU-018-257

TESS HOLLIDAY

The Not So Subtle Art of Being a Fat Girl

LOVING THE SKIN YOU'RE IN

BLINK

bringing you closer

Published by Blink Publishing
3.08, The Plaza,
535 Kings Road,
Chelsea Harbour,
London, SW10 0SZ

www.blinkpublishing.co.uk

facebook.com/blinkpublishing
twitter.com/blinkpublishing

Trade Paperback – 978-1-911274-77-3
eBook – 978-1-911274-78-0

All rights reserved. No part of the publication may be reproduced,
stored in a retrieval system, transmitted or circulated in any form or by
any means, electronic, mechanical, photocopying, recording or otherwise,
without prior permission in writing of the publisher.

A CIP catalogue of this book is available from the British Library.

Designed and set by seagulls.net
Printed and bound by Clays Ltd, St. Ives Plc

1 3 5 7 9 10 8 6 4 2

Copyright © Tess Holliday, 2017
Text written by Charlotte Ward, 2017
Text copyright © Blink Publishing Limited, 2017

Tess Holliday has asserted their moral right to be identified as the author of this
Work in accordance with the Copyright, Designs and Patents Act 1988.

This book reflects the author's recollections of her experiences, and while great
care has been taken to recount all conversations and occurrences faithfully,
some parties may remember events differently. Please note that some names and
identifying details have been changed to protect the privacy of individuals.

Every reasonable effort has been made to trace copyright holders of material
reproduced in this book, but if any have been inadvertently overlooked the
publishers would be glad to hear from them.

Blink Publishing is an imprint of the Bonnier Publishing Group
www.bonnierpublishing.co.uk

This book is for anyone who has ever doubted themselves or the magic that lies within them.

Contents

Introduction

I didn't always love the skin I am in.

Like many of us often do, I cared too much about what other people thought. I let bad people and experiences break me down. I listened to bullies, critics and trolls on the internet. I let cruel, uninvited comments influence how I felt and acted towards other people. I allowed myself to be shamed and set the bar low with my expectations of how I should be treated. There were times when I looked at my body and saw nothing but how flawed I was or wished I could look different. I allowed men to abuse me or put me down. I was too soft with people I loved, too grateful for attention or too willing to let people take advantage of me.

When I look back at my life to date it sometimes feels like a soap opera. It's hard to imagine the rollercoaster that has been my life and everything that has happened, or even my own reactions to it. I've made good and really bad decisions, recoiled and rebelled, procrastinated and just said fuck it and did the best I could. I've felt worthless and beautiful, been timid and outspoken and reserved and reckless. I've felt both beaten down and unstoppable. I still have a lot to learn, but now, as I navigate my thirties, I feel like I'm a little less of a dumpster fire.

I've realized that throughout my life there have been moments that have shaped me into who I am, and people who helped me along the way to get to where I am now. It hasn't been an easy journey and I don't have it all figured out; I don't have all the answers. Hell, half of the time I don't even know what I'm doing – but I can honestly say I am happy of the woman I am today, regardless of what others think.

So this book is for anyone who was told they weren't good enough, for anyone who felt like they didn't matter, that your dreams were too impossible, that you didn't deserve a space in this world because you are 'different'. Sometimes I feel like everyone is looking at me and thinking 'why her?' and I get that. I wonder the same thing sometimes. The reality is, I was born to stand out, to make people question things they thought they knew and to exist fearlessly in a space that we are told bodies like mine don't deserve to be in. I hope when you read this book, you learn a thing or two or take away that you deserve everything you can dream, and maybe take a little advice from the mistakes I've made. I'm here to tell you that the impossible IS possible, YOU matter, and that almost everything is better fried. Time to dig in!

Chapter 1

'Your Dad's an Ass and I'm Leaving Him'

It's hard to talk about my childhood. While my life seems relatively glamorous now, long before I was living out my dreams in Los Angeles as Tess Holliday, I was Ryann Maegen Hoven, the name my parents chose for me and my legal name to this day.

I feel like my mom always did the best she could for my younger brother Tad and me, but you just can't sugarcoat the fact that growing up was, in a lot of ways, pretty terrible for us.

By my ninth birthday, I had moved more times than I can remember and witnessed my parents' marriage reach its inevitable end, due mostly to the fact that my dad was fooling around with anything in a skirt. Still reeling from the upheaval a divorce thrusts upon a family, and just weeks before I turned ten years old, I was told my mom was going to be 'a vegetable' after her boyfriend shot her in the head.

I've told the story so many times now that I have a tendency to phrase it quite bluntly. More often than not it's met with stunned silence and teary eyes. I know it's shocking to hear this stuff and bizarrely it is often me comforting other people as they process it. Sometimes I surprise myself that I can be so emotionally detached after what my family has been through. Looking back, I honestly think I've become kind of numb to it as a way to protect myself. It's hard to remember how some of it made me feel and maybe elements of my childhood are just too painful to recall. I've seen a therapist on and off since I was a kid to help me process it, long before I ended up in LA, where every man and his dog has a therapist. This sounds like a joke but there are literally dog therapists here. Classic la la land!

From a young age my life was simply about surviving. I was dealing with circumstances no child should ever have to deal with and finding a way to keep going no matter what. It taught me to be tough and rely on myself when adults were letting me down.

Later in life when people told me my dreams weren't realistic, I would always think, Really? I've had some of the shittiest things happen to me and survived them. When I look at my life as a whole, carving out a new niche in the modeling world is far from the most ridiculous hurdle I've faced. I've never listened to people trying to limit me and I never will.

I was born in Laurel, Mississippi, in 1985, and finished high school in the same town in 2003. But for the first decade of my life, I lived in a couple of dozen cities in almost as many states.

I don't remember everywhere we lived or why we moved there but I do remember how uneasy it made me feel when suddenly we were uprooted and on the road to a new place.

One of my earliest memories is being in kindergarten and coming home thinking it was just a normal day to find a moving truck outside of our house. That night we just upped and moved to a different city, which is pretty fucked up when you think about it. This set the tone for that period of my young life – I'd just get used to a new school and we'd be off again.

My dad worked for an auto-parts retailer and I remember being told that he would get paid more to move jobs quickly. It's true that he was always a hard worker who was in demand and frequently got promoted, but now that I'm older I'm not so sure that's the whole story. The reality was my dad had several affairs we know about (and surely countless others that we don't) and whether he was following his dick to a new conquest or running from their likely armed and angry husband, I suspect that his cheating might have been the real reason behind our nomadic life. I remember once we moved in the middle of the night.

It seemed to me that Dad always had a pretty fluid concept of the truth, bending it to suit his agenda. Even with the benefit of hindsight it's hard to separate the fact from the fiction.

Like the time we were watching *Forrest Gump* and Dad casually claimed he used to have braces on his legs just like the hero of the film. He always maintained this story was true, despite the fact that there is no photographic evidence and his own family members say it never happened.

By far Dad's most obvious lies were to Mom to cover up his cheating. My father's biggest weakness would always be women and his fraternizing began even before Mom married him. Mom recalls getting a card in the mail a month before their wedding telling her not to marry Dad because he was screwing around.

'Here's my two cents' worth,' the sender had signed off anonymously, next to two pennies taped to the paper. Dad, of course, denied everything. He'd often claim he had to drive into the city for work or that he was off for a weekend 'deer hunting'.

'He said he was hunting four-legged bucks but he was busy chasing two-legged does,' Mom told me later.

I'm not the cheating type, so his motivations are still a mystery to me, but I would think that most men who are cheating on their wives would at least have the good sense not to take their young children with them on a date. Not Dad though – his confidence often strayed into the territory of arrogance – and in that spirit he once took Tad and me to the movies with a woman who now I can only believe was his mistress. I was five years old and Tad was four. When we arrived home I inadvertently outed Dad as I rushed to tell Mom about the 'nice lady' who had taken me to the bathroom at the movie theatre. When Mom questioned why Dad had allowed a complete stranger to accompany his daughter into the restrooms he grew defensive.

'It was just a lady I know from the store,' he claimed. 'I'd never fool around on you, I love you!' He never wavered from the 'deny everything!' defence, and I guess we'll never know for sure.

Mom was no idiot and knew in her heart my father was messing around, but she struggled to find the strength to leave him. Being so far away from her family was hard. Time after time, as they arrived in a new town with no support system, Mom would find herself afraid and overwhelmed. She was isolated with two young children, with friends few and far between. How could she leave now?

There was no doubt their marriage was failing and all four of us were miserable. I can't count how many times screaming matches between my parents escalated to physical fights as Tad and I cowered out of the line of fire of my dad's explosive temper. Crying and begging them to stop only intensified his anger towards my mom. Sometimes he hit us too, taking off his belt and beating us across the ass and legs.

Their worst argument I witnessed I can remember vividly. It ended with Mom on the floor and Dad pushing a wooden dining room chair against her neck. I remember watching my mother gasping for air. Had Mom's friend Susan not been visiting I don't know what would have happened. She intervened and pulled Dad off her before he could do any long term physical damage, though we both wear the mental scars to this day.

When his anger subsided he would be as sweet as pie, playing the part of a remorseful and attentive husband and father until inevitably the volcanic pressure built up again. As I've met women around the world and heard their stories I have come to realize he exhibited a lot of the traits of a classic abuser. I think a big part of his anger problem came from the fact that he just couldn't stomach being criticized and he never faced up to the flaws in his character. He was 19 when I was born, and I imagine it was pretty hard to find himself a parent so young. I can empathize with this as a parent now myself, but still he let me down in my youth. He could not understand that when you commit to something people feel let down when you don't see it through. It seemed to me that his interest in anyone and anything could wane at the drop of a hat.

Tess Holliday's Advice for Life #7:
If someone says they are sorry but
continues the same bad behavior, trust
their actions and not their words.

When he wasn't womanizing and dragging us from shithole to shithole across the South he was collecting (and then discarding) a menagerie of domestic and exotic critters. He claimed he loved animals but in truth he had neither the patience or the compassion for the poor animals that drew the cosmic short straw in meeting my dad.

Once, right before we moved house, he acquired a 'pet' crow – from where, and how, remains a mystery. The poor thing was shoved unceremoniously into a box with holes poked in it, and completely stunk out our moving van. Then there was the very clearly wild rat he found at work and proudly brought home to be our new pet. It lived a sad solitary life in a fish tank aquarium in our front room until the fateful day he told me I could pet it. The rat was obviously not domesticated so when I reached into the tank, naturally is saw me as a threat and bit me. I cried. Without hesitation Dad snatched up the rat and hurled it into the backyard where much to my horror our five pet dogs proceeded to rip it apart. The dogs' fate was slightly better: they lasted until my parents eventually split when they were unceremoniously palmed off on the people who bought our house.

Years later Dad owned a boa constrictor theatrically named Cleopatra. She was his pride and joy until the day she twisted around his waist and squeezed through his jean belt loops. Suddenly Dad was in grave danger of being crushed to death by his pet. He whipped out his pocket knife and cut through the belt hoops to free himself. Perhaps a normal person would have found a new home for the snake but not Dad. He turned the knife on the snake, and cut her head off, and later bitched for weeks about ruining those beloved Tommy Hilfiger jeans. It was a similar fate for a 'miniature pig' that in a turn of events that would surprise absolutely no one, grew too big for its tiny makeshift home in a townhouse pantry, and sadly ended up at the butcher.

* * *

It was 1993 and we were living in Lenoir, North Carolina, when Mom finally told Dad she'd had enough.

That day, after school, Dad instructed Tad and me to sit with him on the couch. His face was like thunder. He'd told Mom it was down to her to break the bad news but he wouldn't allow her to sit with us.

In an act of bravery and defiance, Mom announced, arms folded from across the room, 'Your dad is an ass and I'm leaving him'.

Before Tad and I knew it our house had been sold and I was bidding goodbye to my only friend at the time, my dog Shadow. She looked quite like a wolf but had the heart of a lamb. Mom's plan was to rent another place in Lenoir and raise us by herself. It had taken her ten years to find the courage to kick her abusive husband out – but within 12 months she met the man who almost succeeded in taking her life.

On the day it happened, Tad, eight, and I were staying

with my father at his girlfriend's house in Tennessee. Dad had moved to a different state after he separated from Mom and had wasted no time in finding a new love interest.

Dad of course still couldn't keep his dick in his pants, and in a scene that could be straight out of a *National Lampoon* movie, I remember him behind the wheel speeding down the highway while precariously scribbling down his phone number for an attractive woman in another car who had caught his eye.

As he held the paper up to the window with a twinkling and self-assured smile, it was obvious his new girlfriend (not to mention his children in the back seat) were the furthest thing from his mind. It was all about the thrill of the chase. He was a handsome man who always had good clothes and his hair slicked back with gel so getting attention was easy for him. I can remember him looking in the car mirror and singing, 'I'm so vain', to the tune of the Carly Simon's song. He wasn't even being ironic.

That year we were supposed to be with Dad for the whole of summer break, and he did his best to keep us entertained. There were fun trips to the movies and baseball games but also fits of temper as he lost patience with us. It was probably the first time he'd had to look after us full time without Mom so I'm sure he found it challenging. The threat to send us back to our mother occurred at least once a day so at first, when he said we were driving back to North Carolina, we had no idea if he was for real or not.

'Your mom has fallen and hit her head,' he revealed, ushering us into the back of his girlfriend's minivan. He wouldn't tell us anymore but stopped at the store to buy us toys and coloring books for the ride. We didn't think much of it at the time because he constantly attempted to buy our affection.

Dad sped and drove erratically the entire six hour journey. We arrived to be greeted by the sight of my grandma looking like she'd seen a ghost. It was then we learnt the true reason for our frantic journey – that Mom had been shot at our home. She was in a drug-induced coma following emergency surgery to remove two bullets from her brain.

'The doctors say she probably won't walk or talk again,' Grandma sobbed to my father within our earshot. 'She could be a vegetable.' I wasn't sure what being a vegetable meant but in the South they are mostly brown and soggy and come from a can, so I knew it couldn't possibly be good.

We sat around at the hospital's neighboring Ronald McDonald House, a charity set up to help house family members of those who are hospitalized, and other members of our family began to arrive – my mom's sister Marilyn and her brother Hal. They patted us on the head and shared concerned looks.

I kept my eyes glued to my coloring book as the

grown-ups talked in hushed tones:

'They can't see her like that … No, they're not going back to Tennessee … He wants us to take them … I think he's been drinking …'

My grandma confirmed her suspicion by making him do a basic sobriety test – to walk a straight line – which he quite obviously failed. Eventually a decision appeared to have been made. The next day, it was announced that Tad and I would be heading off to stay with relatives 600 miles away back in Laurel, Mississippi. I would live with Aunt Marilyn while Tad stayed with Uncle Hal. Neither of us knew if we would see our mom again.

* * *

But Mom wasn't a vegetable. Three days after the shooting she woke up. The attack had damaged the left side of her brain, partially paralyzing the right side of her body, but she was able to communicate. She couldn't form her words very clearly but seemed to understand what people were saying to her. She still had her long-term memory, but her short-term memory had been affected. It would be a long journey back to learning how to walk and talk again.

Still scared for her life, she claimed she didn't know who had attacked her. The detectives on the case had a hunch though – they were already suspicious of Mom's boyfriend, Tim, who had been the first person on the scene and raised the alarm. Tim claimed to have 'discovered' Mom lying lifeless in the bath with two bullet wounds to the back of her head after returning home from his job at a furniture factory across the street. After making the grim discovery he ran to the volunteer fire station next door to get help. When the paramedics told him Mom was still breathing, the color drained from his face.

While the house had all the hallmarks of a home invasion – a severed phone line and stolen jewelry – it was obvious to police that the windows had been smashed from the inside out. Then there was Mom's reaction when Tim came to the hospital to visit her. He was her boyfriend of almost a year but when he leaned across the bed to touch her toes she recoiled in terror. Tim was arrested and Mom began to reveal the full, horrible details of her attack to a kindly female police officer.

On the morning of Mom's attempted murder, Tim had pretended to be sick and stayed in bed. As she got ready for work he'd pulled the covers up to his neck.

'I'm staying home today,' he told her. 'I've got a killer headache.'

Mom said she went to the bathroom and was preparing to shower when she heard a noise in the hallway. Through the gap in the door she saw Tim lurking with a handgun. She immediately slammed the door shut and tried to lock it but Tim forced his way in.

'Get into the bathtub,' he told her. 'Turn around and face the wall.'

For a crazy moment Mom thought he was going to

shoot himself but then she heard ringing in her ears and knew she had been shot. For six hours she drifted in and out of consciousness and had visions of all four of her deceased grandparents. She says that they sat vigil with her, as clear as day, sitting around the bathtub singing church hymns to keep her going.

'They walked me through my memories and I believe they were guiding me to the next life,' she says. 'But then the paramedics arrived and I got a second chance.'

When she finally reached hospital, hours and hours after the shooting, things didn't look good. When the doctors set to work trying to remove the bullet fragments they had no idea if she would live or die. The surgery left a grizzly looking incision on the back of her neck. When Tad and I finally got to visit our mother, ten days after her attack, it was the first thing we wanted to see.

When we walked into her hospital room Mom was sitting in a wheelchair. She looked different. The shooting had paralyzed the right side of her face, and although she tried to act as naturally as she could so as not to scare us, it was immediately apparent that on top of not being able to walk her right arm was almost immobile. Like many people with brain injuries she needed to relearn the simplest of tasks and had a grueling year ahead of intense physical therapy and occupational therapy to get her mobility back.

She was wearing a blue denim hat to hide the full extent of her injuries from her children. It was folded up at the front with a flower on it, and was not something Mom would normally wear.

I suddenly felt very shy, like I was approaching someone I didn't know very well.

'I'm sorry I have this stupid hat on,' Mom said, breaking the ice with an eye roll. Her voice was muffled and slurred, like a drunk with a mouthful of late night fast food.

'Here,' she said, thrusting a soft, stuffed cat into my hand with her good arm.

'I had to get you this cat,' she said with distaste. 'It's all the gift shop had.'

I laughed because Mom hated cats. Even though my aunt had told me that I needed to be strong for her and the family, I couldn't hold back my tears.

Once I'd got over the initial shock of Mom's appearance I started to peer curiously at her shaved head. Her skin was a rainbow of colors from bruising and the various disinfectants the doctors had put on it.

'Can we look?'

She sighed and stoically instructed the nurse: 'Take my hat off.'

Tad and I stared open-mouthed at the damage in the way only kids can, swapping perversely excited side-glances as we checked out the gore. There was a big scar running down the back of my mom's neck and 32 staples!

'There's a bullet still in there!' Mom said.

That was the last time we saw Mom for a while.

While she was recuperating in hospital my family cleared out our house and we remained in Mississippi, 600 miles away. The shooting had left Mom permanently disabled so there was no way she could go back to Lenoir. When she did get out of hospital she was taken by ambulance to Laurel. The three of us moved into my grandparents' place while Mom continued her rehabilitation.

My mother faced her situation with a steely determination. She continued to go to physical therapy to build her strength and regain the movement in her face. By now she was walking, but would tire easily and often felt dizzy. She took her wheelchair wherever she went. The bullet fragments in her head caused her almost constant pain but she would stubbornly insist on doing most things herself and rarely asked for help.

'I didn't die because I am hard-headed,' she'd joke, and there is probably an element of truth in that. There is more than a little of that spirit in me, and it's part of what made me never give up, not only in my personal life but in my career.

Mom's disability drastically changed all of our lives but she made an unwavering effort in every way she could to be a 'regular mom'. She would insist on driving my brother and me everywhere and on good days she would even go walking with us. Now that she couldn't work we didn't have much money but we got by with disability payments, help from my grandparents and the church community and child support reluctantly given up by my dad. We didn't get all of the nice stuff that everyone else got but my mom always made sure we were loved and well taken care of.

* * *

What happened to my mom and the fallout from that situation definitely changed me forever. From a young age, I understood that the world could be a dangerous and ugly place. It made me see that relationships can be toxic and it influenced the way I view love and friendships. I struggled to make friends, and still find it hard to really trust people. When you have been so vulnerable as a child it is instinctive to put up walls. I am still working on that.

It's hard for me to say but I think Mom knew deep down that Tim was not a good person. Like my father, Tim had a temper and once pushed Tad down the stairs in a fit of rage all because he could not find the television remote control. We told Mom at the time but she thought we were exaggerating. I think she found it hard to accept that after all she'd been through with Dad she had chosen another man with a dark side. She is kind and compassionate but has an innate need to find people and fix them. She learnt the hard way to protect her heart. Now if my husband Nick and I ever get into a heated argument in front of her I see the fear in her eyes. She panics and tells me, 'You have to leave him! It won't get any better!' Then she apologizes, saying, 'I'm sorry, I am projecting.'

It has meant I am often unable to ask my mom for relationship advice. She is a good person with a good heart but she has had too much trauma in her life to be objective.

I never blamed my mom for what happened to her (and by consequence to us) because she was young and when you're young and infatuated you don't always understand that abuse is not the norm.

Growing up with a violent father and seeing what my mom went through also made me wary of the warning signs. I think that is why I am so outspoken now about loving yourself. It is never acceptable for anyone to belittle or intimidate you in a relationship, let alone lay a hand on you. While we may be inclined to love unconditionally, when people you love let you down then you have to dig deep and find your inner strength.

Tess Holliday's Advice for Life #12: Love shouldn't damage you.

When I was 27 I decided to permanently cut ties with my dad. It was part of me deciding not to let people in my life who don't treat me well. Over the years I gave him so many chances but I was always the one putting in the effort and just not getting much back. I was tired of him always being a jerk. I guess I realized that I didn't have to give him that power over me any more. He doesn't try to get in touch. He has sent my oldest son one Christmas gift in his entire life, so even though it makes me sad I don't think he and his little brother are missing out on much. I see now that our lives are better without my dad in it.

I think in his own way Dad loved me, but the same patterns of behavior came up over and over again. In my teens he contributed to some very negative thoughts about myself. I will never forget some of the hurtful things he said and did.

As a parent myself I know that you have a responsibility to be a role model. You have to be the bigger person (no pun intended). If I find myself getting upset or losing patience with my children, I try to check myself. I ask myself the hard question: 'Am I being like my mom or dad? How would I have felt about this as a child? How will my children look back at this situation? How can I make sure they feel secure and loved?'

At the same time, I'm not one to gloss over things. I still remember how helpless and uninformed I felt during the aftermath of my mom's attack. Not knowing is often worse than facing a hard truth. If my eleven-year-old asks me a difficult question I don't shy away from answering it. We've had candid talks about lots of things. I want to prepare him for a complex world where he'll need to find his own feet. He and his brother *will* learn about survival and endurance – just hopefully without the pain and suffering I endured as a child.

I think that experiencing such adversity so young has meant that I have a tendency to fear the worst and I'm always ready to dive into survival mode. I know that I sometimes create problems that aren't there, fixate on the worse-case scenario or start to get overwhelmed. At other times I know I should be freaking out but I can't. The shutters just go down and I am eerily calm.

Either way, I have to remind myself to relax and breathe. Life isn't always out to get you. Yes, it may be a fickle bitch, but even when times are tough, there is always hope and things change quickly. You have to persevere and keep on trying until there is nothing else to do. Keep enduring and moving forward. Actively make things better for yourself and others. Fight for what you want. You can do it.

Chapter 2

Bible Belt: Size Extra Large

When I look back to my tween years it's clear I already had my own unique sense of style and identity. Brightly colored t-shirts covered in smiley, acid faces were the shit for me. I loved everything 1990s and hung around in baggy jeans and customized band tees. I was really into acrylic dresses, à la Baby Spice, which I accessorized with tattoo chokers and charm bracelets. I cringe a little at seeing most of these trends return, but you can pry my chokers from my cold, dead, chunky hands.

At age ten I had exactly the same attitude to clothes I have now. If I like it, I am going to wear it. There are no rules. I expressed myself through fashion and did my own thing.

Tess Holliday's Advice for Life #25:
Fashion doesn't have to be serious!
Don't be afraid to express yourself.

Like lots of things in life, the fundamental knowledge of how to be was already there inside me. All I had to do was answer the questions from my heart: What makes you happy? What do you want to do? What do you really want to wear? Why would you want to be like everyone else?

Deep down I knew it was way more fun to stand out than it was to fit in. It shows you have something to say and your own perspective of the world. If I saw that odd little girl now I'd give her a hug and a high five. I wish she had held on to that freewheeling attitude to life, but I feel like somewhere around 10 or 11 children switch to high alert to single out the misfits. School tribes are formed with the cool kids ruling the roost and a cruel hierarchy that labels anyone 'awkward' or 'different' as the class loser.

When I enrolled at elementary school in Laurel in 1995 I was already feeling emotionally battered and bruised. My family had just been through hell and all I wanted was to blend into the background. For most of my life I'd been the new kid, arriving in new towns seemingly at my father's whim and having to join a new school and class. At every new school the teacher would introduce me and a sea of faces would examine me quizzically. I knew I would have that moment of feeling uncomfortable in my skin, not knowing what to do with my arms or where to look. Mostly I'd just gaze at the floor and then shuffle to my assigned desk. That was just the way it was.

There would be the familiar stress of finding my locker and the restrooms and knowing where to sit in the school cafeteria. I hated that feeling. Going through this time and time again didn't make me any more accomplished at making friends. I dreaded putting myself out there and hoping someone would befriend me. To this day I still find it hard to let new people in.

The reality was that even if I did make new friends we were always moving and I would rarely get to see them again. I often wonder what my childhood would have been like if I'd had Skype and Facebook. Perhaps leaving friends behind would be easier and the distance and isolation less harsh with modern technology to bridge the gap.

My mom, being kind, always did her best to stay in touch with the bunch of misfits I'd managed to collect as friends. She would exchange information with the other mothers and tried to keep up with the comings and goings of the families.

One day when I was seven, I arrived home from school in Navarre, Florida, to find Mandy, my best friend, waiting for me in my bedroom. Mom had arranged for her to travel five hours from Ocala, Florida, to visit us, along with Jeremy, a friend of my brother. That day, as I caught up with Mandy, it felt like I had won the lottery. Mom took us to see the Easter Bunny and I can remember vividly how happy I felt. I still treasure the photo of Mandy and me sitting on his knee.

Whenever I recall that special day it is a reminder to make memories with my sons. I always think, 'Is this the thing he's always going to remember? How can I make it the best memory possible?'

When we arrived back in my birthplace of Laurel I'd hoped my 'new girl' days were over. Ever since the attack Mom had relied on her parents for help so we'd moved into my grandparents' tiny two-bedroomed house on their 25-acre homestead. The land had been passed down from my maternal great-grandparents and had once been a working farm with horses, cows and huge garden crops.

My grandfather, or Paw Paw as I called him, kept up a small garden growing peas, butterbeans, corn, okra, tomatoes, squash, cucumber and eggplants, but now the land mostly consisted of fields left to pasture. There was also a pond filled with giant catfish and a log cabin for camping.

Even in the tightest knit family, five people living on top of each other and sharing one bathroom was not going to work long term, so my grandfather purchased a singlewide trailer from a friend. He also bought Mom a battered old Ford to get around. He set the trailer in the middle of an old cow pasture a few minutes' walk from the farmhouse and we furnished it with donated gifts from the local church or family.

As trailers went it was not bad at all. The three of us had a bedroom each and two bathrooms. There was a box air conditioning unit attached to a window to keep us cool and fans in our rooms. Living in the middle of a field meant that although it was nice to be close to nature, the occasional mouse or cockroach liked to visit. It was a simple, cozy time in our lives. I loved picking honeysuckle, pulling off the stem that held the petals together and sucking out the nectar. As dusk fell over the neighboring woods I would watch the fireflies as they produced tiny frenetic sparks of flourescent green. They were so magical, dancing in the warm evening air. Tad and I would catch them in jars just to look at them. You kind of take them for granted until you live somewhere that doesn't have them.

I would visit my grandparents' house every single day salivating as my grandma, or Maw Maw as we call her, rustled up Southern homemade delights. Chicken and dumplings with butterbeans, sweet potatoes and dinner rolls. Carb heavy, buttery comfort food. Those meals always felt like a hug, and I'm sure contributed in no small part to both my ongoing love of food and my ample ass.

Hanging out at Maw and Paw's was always fun – apart from when I was in trouble. During the winter season, Mom's punishment of choice was to send us into the yard to pick up pecans. The pecan tree had been planted by my great-grandmother and was our family's pride and joy. Sadly it didn't survive Hurricane Katrina, but for many years it bore a steady harvest of pecan nuts that my mother would use to bake pecan pies, Mississippi mud cake and chocolate chip, wedding or cherry wink cookies. My grandmother also loved to toast them with sugar.

It would take ages to fill a brown paper bag full of pecans but I would make the task last as long as I could. I would sit on the ground, bundled up in a cardigan, and pick up nuts in a circle around me, enjoying the peace and quiet. It was almost meditative to me. Sometimes I would sing or think of a life far away. My imagination was crazy growing up and I quite often lived in my head, wrapped up in my thoughts. It's part of what got me through what would have otherwise often been a lonely existence.

Since our return to Laurel we had been welcomed into my grandparents' Southern Baptist church. Being a member of the church community brought Mom a lot of peace and purpose. Whether it was offering meals, repairing our porch or thinking of us in their prayers the congregation rallied round to help our family.

In the South, faith and education are closer together than my thighs, so religion also extended into my school life. Every day at school when we stood and placed our hands on our hearts to recite the Pledge of Allegiance we would also list the Ten Commandments and salute the Christian flag.

While this was the norm for me I think it was at this age that I first began to question some of the things I was being taught – or rather that were being omitted from my education. I just wasn't learning what other kids learnt. Facts of basic science and world history were being overlooked. I did not know much that was happening outside the South. It was a twisted version of reality.

Just like any inquisitive kid I naturally heard about things such as dinosaurs, cavemen and space. But not at school. They did not teach kids about evolution or the Big Bang. God had created the universe (in seven days no less – #overacheiver) and that was all there was to it. But when the television news reported that archeologists in far flung corners of the globe had discovered dinosaur bones it left me confused. Where did that fit into what I was learning?

When I asked Mom about dinosaurs she bluntly told me that they weren't real. 'It wasn't in the Bible,' she said.

Unsatisfied with her answer I would ask more questions. I wanted to know where the fossils of dinosaurs and other prehistoric creatures had come from if they weren't real. My questions were dismissed both at home and at school: 'Don't question it, trust in God'. As far as they were concerened, if it wasn't in the Bible then it wasn't true.

When you are hearing these things from people who love you it is hard to protest too much. Why would they tell me something untrue? I know now that it is a lack of education that makes people think this way. But as a child I learnt not to argue too much. For some people the culture bubble that is the South is all they will ever know. I always knew it wasn't enough for me. I dreamed of what life might be like outside of Mississippi, and although I had very little knowledge of the world beyond the South I knew there had to be more than this.

When JK Rowling's *Harry Potter* books came out, there was a strong push in the church community that books about magic were 'satanic' and could pollute the minds of kids. Although my Mom was living her life to the letter of the Bible, she had the good sense to dismiss those claims, which is just as well as I grew to be a big fan of the series. It was a beautiful escape for me to be wrapped up in a magical world, far away from my little life.

* * *

When I started in the fifth grade at Shady Grove Elementary School it didn't take long to get the lowdown on the playground. All the popular guys were football players and had that jock mentality of making everyone else's lives miserable for their own entertainment. The popular girls were cheerleaders with names like Lindsey, Britney and Jenny. They had swishy, shiny hair worn up in perfect ponytails with big bows. I had a 'boy's name', a short haircut to match, and a fondness for anything Tweety Bird that made me chronically uncool. I would need to work to make friends, but even at the tender age of ten I knew the worst thing I could do was try *too hard*. Nothing repels kids more than the smell of desperation. One drop of blood in the water and the sharks will circle. I spent my first day trying unsuccessfully to look nonchalant in class and carefree during recess when really I was feeling stressed and lonely.

To make things even harder, it was clear that a lot of the kids at my new school came from rich families. In the South a lot of families are born into money, either old oil money or from traditional family professions like medicine passed down from father to son. There was a big divide between the rich and the poor in the town and it appeared what you wore could seal your fate in an instant. The popular kids had the latest Nikes or branded clothing but I was making do with budget and church-donated versions. I feared that the other kids could tell my clothes were hand-me-downs or from Baby Showcase, the clothing store in Laurel where my Grandma worked. Even if they didn't know I lived in a trailer my clothes would give me away. I was right to be concerned, I would get bullied for my clothes. However, first my peers found an altogether crueler reason to ridicule me – my disabled mother.

'What's wrong with your mom? She looks weird,' a boy with ginger hair asked me on my first week of school. He said it loudly so the kids around us would hear and laugh. I didn't answer him and walked away. I didn't know it then but he would go on to be one of my most prolific playground tormentors. If you're reading this, I forgive you, and I understand that many kids bully because they are being bullied themselves or have a crappy home life, but I'm still going to kick you in the nuts if we ever cross paths. It's only fair.

The comment about my mom left me embarrassed but it also made me channel my anger in an irrational direction. If I'm honest, in that moment I resented my mom for making me vulnerable to bullying. I resented that kids at school thought it was funny she was in a wheelchair and I resented that I was poor. Of course neither of these things were my mom's fault but who said children are logical? I wanted so badly to fit in and I was annoyed to be tainted by association. Despite feeling very sorry for myself I could never bring myself to tell my mom that people were talking shit about her. Deep down I knew that none of this was really her fault. It would be pretty low to hurt her and I'm glad I never did.

That experience set the tone for my entire time at school. Barely a day would pass without a cruel comment directed at me in the hallway or playground.

'Oh my God look at your shoes!'

'Is your mom a retard?'

'What's it like being so poor?'

'Your outfit is so ugly.'

I was too embarrassed to fight back or retaliate. Instead I'd walk away, heading off to sit on a bench by myself. It was there, as I drowned my sorrows in a bag of Cheetos, that I was first insulted about my body.

A predisposition to comfort eat combined with the genetically inherited body type of my mom – big butt, strong thighs and large arms – meant that puberty hit me hard and fast. Before the age of 11 I had started to get boobs and put on weight.

It was right after my mom got shot that I'd started to comfort eat. During those first few terrible days when it was uncertain whether I would see her again, I remember feeling like I was just going through the motions – I played with Cabbage Patch Dolls and watched *Jeopardy* with my aunt, I said please and thank you and went to bed without making a fuss. I didn't want to be a nuisance, but inside I was drowning in an ocean of fear and panic. I didn't understand what was happening to my mother and I could not confide in my aunt. My family didn't talk much about feelings.

'It's not polite to burden people,' Maw always said. Her generation had lived through the Second World War and were used to being stoney faced in the wake of adversity. There was no doubt my extended family loved me but it never occurred to them to encourage me to express my emotions even in such a time of tragedy.

For a while, I had a hard time expressing myself because my family frowned upon it. I realize now that bottling things up does no good at all. Expressing your problems is better than suppressing them because you're actually dealing with the shit in your life. When it's all out there you can start looking for solutions. I've definitely become more outspoken about my feelings over the years and I am much more honest with my boys than my family ever were with me as a kid. I know from my own experiences that not being told the whole truth only makes things more complicated. Kids are way more resilient than we give them credit for.

But back then my mom was the only person I could, or wanted to talk to. I felt lost without her. My only release from this state of perpetual panic was when Aunt Marilyn placed a bowl of Campbell's vegetable beef soup in front of me. I love soup. It is one of my favorite things to eat so for a moment I felt happy. I dipped my spoon in and swirled it.

Aunt Marilyn passed me a packet of crackers so I tipped the box and stirred in a handful of flakes. I started to eat, enjoying the buttery goodness of the crackers and savory taste of the soup. Then I raided the packet again and stirred in some more. I did this again and again until the entire packet of crackers was in my bowl. It was more soggy crackers than it was soup, but it was so delicious and comforting.

From that day onwards I think I instinctively turned to food for comfort. Food was my release, a way to temporarily forget my problems, but it also led to weight gain.

Tess Holliday's Advice for Life #27:
It's fine to eat your feelings, but guac is extra.

As a kid I'd never thought about my body type or weight. I'd spent hot summers running around the garden naked without a care in the world. But suddenly my body was up for discussion; it could be used as a weapon to insult me.

For a young girl still happy to play with Barbies, it was alarming to have womanhood unceremoniously thrust upon me. The cute short shorts and fitted tops Grandma had got me from Baby Showcase, didn't fit anymore: I suddenly had boobs, hips and a butt. My tops grew tight and my pants uncomfortable. I was self-conscious at my blossoming body.

'We'll go to JC Penney,' Mom said.

It was there she bought me a bra. A scary contraption that was a far cry from the cute and comfy Smurfs training bra she'd got me when I was six. This new grown-up bra had uncomfortable straps and gave me backache. Next Mom helped me picked out a pair of jeans. I was surprised that I needed an adult US size 12.

'I don't know what to tell you,' Mom said. 'You have a big butt, like me.'

I found the changes to my body embarrassing and alarming. I asked Mom about the little crinkly lines I had spotted on my stomach.

'They're stretchmarks,' Mom said.

'Will I have them forever?' I asked.

'Yes,' she replied. 'They're just a normal part of being a woman.'

Despite her reassurance, I hated those lines. I smothered them with anything that I heard might help but it made little difference.

These days when I look at my body I have many more stretch marks but rather than hate them I see them as a badge of honor. They remind me how amazing my body – which has grown and nurtured two children – really is.

Tess Holliday's Advice for Life #32:
Stretch marks are totally normal.
Everyone has them. Chill.

At the time, though, insults about my developing body were constant.

Disgusting.

Fatso.

Fat ass.

'It's Ryann the Rhino,' my awful little bully declared as I boarded the school bus, prompting fits of laughter from the kids around us. I shrunk down in my seat trying not to cry.

The sad thing is he was clearly trying to deflect the attention from his own predicament of being different. After being persecuted with insults such as 'carrot top', 'freckle face' and 'ginger' he had turned persecutor. Actually, no, don't feel sorry for him, he was a dickhead.

There is a lot of pressure on kids to be cool and to be in with the in-crowd so it wasn't just the ginger kid who picked on me. Other children insulted me in the hallways and more than one delivered poison-pen notes to my locker. Sometimes when I was in the bathroom I'd overhear girls talking about me, calling me gross or fat. I'd pull my feet up so they couldn't see it was me, and sob silently until they left. The evil little shits even put hate mail in my mailbox at home. The insults were scribbled on pieces of paper and although I don't remember what they said I remember how they made me feel. Whenever I spotted anything handwritten folded amongst the bills and junk mail I'd know it was for me. My heart would start to race and I would feel a sense of dread. It was awful.

I know now that even nice kids can succumb to peer pressure to be mean to the 'less cool' kids because they are scared of being singled out or bullied themselves. It's just a shame that my classmates were prepared to throw me under the bus because of their need to fit in.

Tess Holliday's Advice for Life #41:
Being silent in the face of bullying is choosing the side of the bully. Support the people around you.

'You just have to ignore them,' Mom advised at the time. 'There is nothing wrong with you. They are just jealous of you.'

Bless my mom. I appreciated her words but I knew there was no way in hell they were jealous of me. Mom's other suggestion was to 'pray on it'. Ever since her near-death experience my mother had become super-religious. The Southern Baptist church we attended was right next to my school and Mom lived her life according to the

Bible. She was sure God had the answer for me and that everything happened for a reason. But I didn't want to hedge my bets on the power of prayer and a divine intervention. I needed a quicker solution, I needed to stop crying myself to sleep.

As well as praying for my suffering to end, Mom agreed to talk to my teachers. I hoped they'd step in and come to my rescue but I'm sad to tell you nothing changed. I told my caregivers ALL the time that the other kids were making my life hell but they did nothing. That still makes me mad.

If that happened now to someone my son's age, I feel like the schools know they will be held to account if they fail to act. When my older son came home one day with marks on him from being hit by bullies, I took the day off and went to the school. The principal was in a meeting and I sat there until he saw me. I cussed him out and he was moved into a new class with a new teacher the very next day. The bullying stopped there.

The only downfall now is that playground bullying has spread to the digital world, following kids home and penetrating their lives in different forms through social media, email and text messages. And it doesn't end with childhood either! Now that I am famous hardly a day goes by without someone writing something nasty about me on my Twitter, Facebook or Instagram pages. I have come to realize that trolling is what unhappy people do.

Tess Holliday's Advice for life #48:
No person who is content with their life
wastes time on their phone or computer
bitching about other people.

At first the comments directed towards me online affected me greatly. Whenever someone said something mean I would obsess over it. It would give me a sick feeling in my stomach, ruin my day and affect my relationships with the people I love. Eventually I asked myself why I was giving these strangers the power to hurt me. I could choose not to be affected. My happiness did not depend on them. What I say now to my critics is that making fun of my body will never fix the void YOU feel within yourself or the issues YOU have when you look in the mirror. The real issue isn't that I'm fat, or my size, it's that you are scared of seeing someone who is happy AND fat. I don't need to be 'fixed' because I'm not the broken one. You are projecting your own problems on to others. Close your mouth and open your heart. Instead of bullying others try working on yourself. What is making YOU unhappy and angry?

Parents need to talk about it and give kids on both sides of the equation the support they need. As well as supporting the kids being bullied I really believe that you have to work with the ones dishing it out as well. What is wrong with them? What is going on at their house? It's hard to know what the answer is but undoubtedly kids who go through this need protection and support and above all to be taken seriously by their teachers.

* * *

As I steeled myself for another hard school year Mom had a rescue plan. During the summer of 1996 she persuaded my father to help fund my tuition for a local private Christian school. Tad, who was in the school year below me and had a great reputation as the class clown, would be going as well, despite protesting the move loudly at every given opportunity.

I was optimistic my life would be better at this new school. My good vibes quickly dissolved when I realized the twelve kids in my new class had known each other forever. They largely came from rich families and were just as judgmental as the snobby kids at my last school. While my perennially popular brother quickly settled into school life, the boys in my class began to call me fat and the girls taunted me when I couldn't run fast in PE. If only they could see the breakneck speeds my fat ass gets up to now to catch the ice cream truck for my boys. No shame!

After a few weeks I finally made a friend, a sweet girl called Brooke who always saved a seat for me. She had slightly bucked teeth but was tall, skinny and pretty, with long black hair and freckles. Brooke didn't seem to care that I was a geek who wore shirts emblazoned with smiley faces on dress-down Fridays. We hung out outside of school a lot talking about our mutual love of the Spice Girls.

Tess Holliday's Advice for Life #50:
I really really really wanna Zig a zig ahh.

When I spent time with her it really didn't matter that everyone else thought I was fat and weird.

Most days at school I was counting down the hours until I could leave and I struggled to apply myself. Unfortunately, while I scooped first place in a school art contest it was not enough to make up for everything I failed that first semester. Flunking out was not acceptable for a private school that prided itself on academia. Halfway through my school year my mother was summoned to see the principal. He told her that I was performing at such a low level that I'd have to leave. My brother could stay but I was out. Once more Mom made the decision to move us both. Tad loved our new school and quickly blamed me for yet again 'ruining his life'.

'It's not my fault you're so stupid,' he ranted. 'I hate you.'

For a while I thought my brother was right – my grades were bad because I was dumb. But actually that's not correct. I was unmotivated, yes, but stupid? No.

Like a lot of children I craved encouragement and consistency. Years of upheaval and bullying made me retreat into myself. When the other kids picked on me I found it hard to focus. I shut down and was not open to learning. All I wanted each day was to go home and hide from the world. My stint at the private school had only made things worse.

I returned to Shady Grove in early 1997 to complete sixth grade, where my *Groundhog Day* hell resumed with daily insults hurled at me as I sat on my trusty bench at recess.

'Look at those thunder thighs,' the ginger boy sung out to his friends as they swaggered past me in the playground. 'You better be careful or you'll break the bench!'

I felt completely worthless. I needed all the support I could get from my parents: some lessons in self-love, some words of encouragement. My mother was hot on this, constantly reminding me that she'd named me Ryann because I was 'unique', but sadly I did not get the same words of encouragement from my dad.

While most fathers suddenly find themselves busy when the subject of their daughter's changing body arises, my dad was very vocal about this embarrassing stage of my life. Tad and I would stay with him every other weekend and one day, as we headed to the movies, he gave me 'his advice' about my untapped sex appeal.

'You're pretty, you've got big ol' boobs and a big ol' butt, but if you lost weight, damn! You could be so sexy!'

Having my blossoming figure criticized and objectified, particularly by him, just didn't feel right. I remember being uncomfortable, but at the time I don't think I really understood how inappropriate my father's comments were.

* * *

In June 1997 when the school year finally ended, I was relieved to bid farewell for good to Shady Grove Elementary School. The following August I would be going to West Jones High School where I hoped to start over. All the same kids would be there but the school was bigger and I was planning to start anew with a positive attitude. I vowed to try a sport in an attempt to get fit and make friends.

By now Mom had remarried, a guy called Bill, who she had known since I was an infant and who had always had a crush on her. Although it was good to see her happy and supported, he personally gave me the creep.

I tried not to feel dismayed that my brother and I would be sharing her attention with her new husband. She was still an attentive mom, always doing thoughtful things like a bringing a cooler with bottles of cold water and snacks when she picked us up from school.

It was that summer as Tad and I cannonballed into the water at Dad's apartment complex that my self-esteem was dealt a final killer blow. I was having a glorious day at the pool, splashing around in the water and giggling with Tad about our father's offensively tiny blue speedos. It was so much fun belly flopping into the water and making up synchronized swimming routines, but before the day was out I would vow never to wear a bathing suit again.

'I'm thinking of joining the swim team!' I confided to Dad that afternoon as I clambered out the water and lay down happy and carefree on a sun lounger. I had never loved sports but I wanted to get into something. Dad had taught me to swim and it was one of my all-time favorite activities. Perhaps I would be good on the team? My father disagreed.

'Don't you think you should lose weight first?' he said looking me up and down pointedly. 'You're a little big for the swim team.'

The criticism flawed me. Feeling embarrassed I covered my torso with a towel. If my father thought size 16 was too big for the swim team what must everyone else think? Suddenly a powerful sense of shame over-ruled any need to enjoy myself or do something I loved. After that, for at least a decade, I would not go anywhere near a pool or a beach.

I was already being teased for my weight at school so being fat shamed by my father had a big effect on me. After that I assumed I was too big to do any kind of sport so I never tried. Soccer was another sport I wanted to try but now felt too embarrassed to set myself up for failure or ridicule. It took until my mid-twenties to shake off those feelings.

In hindsight, maybe my father thought he was sparing my feelings—maybe he wanted to protect me from mean kids on the team—but in truth he was devastating me. For any parents out there who think they're shielding their children by shaming them, you can actually do a lot of harm. It's not fair to project your insecurities onto your children. Now as a parent I am very careful not to react in a negative way when my older son tells me he wants to do something. I am very aware that when you are a child of abuse you can fall into the same patterns so I always try to encourage him to do whatever he wants. Whether that's breakdancing on a whim or thinking he'll be the next Kobe Bryant I tell him, 'If you want to try it you can do it.'

I am sure my dad tried to be a decent father but he just wasn't very good at it. When I moved to Seattle aged 18 and saw the relationship between my friend Heather and her father it really opened my eyes. Her dad was loving and supportive and never commented on her body or sexuality. It would make me think back to my own home environment and how I was made to cover up my body because of my size—I was told that I was making other people uncomfortable. Now as a parent being naked in our house is not frowned upon or taboo, but we are clear to make the distinction that bodies aren't inherently sexual. There is nothing wrong with being comfortable in your naked body.

Tess Holliday's Advice for Life #55:
Nudity is not inherently sexual. Be nude with
your friends, it's bonding and liberating!

Living with Heather's family I began to see that what my dad did and said were not normal. He was vain by nature and very narcissistic and put a lot of value on looks. I think in some ways he just could not stand that I was growing up to have a figure just like my mom's. Perhaps he didn't realize that making derogatory remarks about my looks had a powerful impact. But like most teenage girls I was very susceptible to negative comments about my body. Being on the receiving end of criticism and bullying make you feel like there is something wrong with you. I wanted to fit in so badly but I was constantly being told I was not good enough at school AND at home. It made me feel embarrassed and sad and like I needed to change.

Sometimes in life I still feel like the underdog but I try to turn that into empowerment. Being different is OK and we should celebrate that in the people around us. These days I speak up a lot about things I find unjust. When I see someone being treated unfairly because they are different I will say something. I am raising my boys to be like that too. I hope that they will never be afraid of breaking away from the status quo to help someone out who needs a friend. Not so long ago I discovered that my older son was using all the spare money he had left over from getting lunch to buy a boy from a disadvantaged family at school something to eat. I felt so proud of him for caring. More people should help others when they are in need.

As he negotiates his tween years, he is already coming home with tales of power battles in the playground as he and his peers tussle to find their place in the world. When he gets picked on I remind him that it is OK to be weird and not to fit in. And that the freckles they pick on him for are now a trend that people are paying huge sums of money to tattoo on their face!

I tell him that although I once hated being 'different', now it is not only my trademark, it's part of how I earn my living. I've learnt that it is hard to knock someone down when they are unashamedly authentic. When you are true to yourself and unapologetic, people (at least the people who really matter) will respect and see you are being genuine.

Tess Holliday's Advice for Life #63:
Embrace what makes you, you.

Chapter 3

F**k 'Em

My teenage years continued to be a crash course in learning to be strong. I was hardly the only fat kid at my school but barely a day passed without a nasty comment flung my way on the bus or in the school corridor. I've never been very good at hiding my emotions but most of the time I'd try to ignore the insults or pretend I hadn't heard.

'Fuck 'em!' I thought, channeling the words of Mom's best friend Tina, who she had known since childhood. Tina was similar to my mom in some ways – they were both so warm and expressive. But she didn't go to church, had a filthy mind and mouth and was completely un-apologetic. Tina was as loud and brash as she looked in her sweatpants. You could spot her coming a mile away thanks to her colorful array of nylon jogging suits, always accessorized with a skinny gold chain, earrings up her ears and a ton of rings. Several years earlier she and Mom had cemented their friendship with matching yin yang tattoos. Though they didn't have a strong grasp on the culture from which it originated, to them it symbolized how they were polar opposites but worked well together.

When Mom encouraged me to pray on my problems, Tina would interrupt.

'They're just jealous of your titties,' she'd announce.

'Tina!' Mom would start to protest.

'No, shut the fuck up, Beth,' Tina would reply. 'I'll say what I want to say. Your daughter needs to hear it. Damn it Ryann, if I had those titties I would be smooshing them in everyone's face. I would be motorboating everyone.' Tina was crude, shocking and completely herself at all times. She never failed to make my mother laugh. Mom often didn't openly approve of what she was saying but she would always smile as she shook her head.

Tina wasn't the only controversial member of her family. Her older brother Roger, who lived in a neighboring trailer, was an openly gay man in a community that largely viewed homosexuality as a one-way ticket to eternal damnation. According to our church, people like Roger were actively sinning by 'choosing' to be gay. The logic of this was lost on me. Why would anyone 'choose' to make life so much harder for themselves? I thought at that age. Even then I understood that being gay is not a choice.

'If religion loves everyone with respect, then surely God loves Roger too,' I decided.

Roger might have been a 'sinner' but he was also a lot of fun. When Tad and I visited him in his trailer he made us corn dog nuggets and put on a movie called *To Wong Foo, Thanks for Everything! Julie Newmar*. This nineties comedy stars Wesley Snipes, Patrick Swayze, and John Leguizamo as three drag queens traveling across the USA experiencing highs and lows. It was my first introduction to drag and gay culture and far from being shocked it changed my life. I loved the glamorous make-up and that the drag queens were so over the top and beautiful. I struggled to understand why anyone wouldn't want to be around these fabulous people.

Why couldn't we just let people be what they wanted to be? I think that's why I am so vocal about telling people that my body is my business. Who you choose to be or love is no one's business but your own. Everyone should live and let live. Yet my mom and me still fight about it. A week before I had Bowie we got into a heated argument after she referred to Caitlyn Jenner as 'It'.

'People should be supported in changing their gender if that is how they feel inside,' I told her.

'That's fine,' she said. 'But you are going to burn in hell.'

See you there I guess, all my beautiful trans brothers and sisters!

Tess Holliday's Advice for Life #69:
LGBT rights are human rights. Sexuality
and gender is a broad and varied spectrum.
All identities are valid.

Most of the time we just don't discuss it any more. I know that is a popular belief in the South and it is just ignorance as far as I am concerned. I don't care about your justifications, religious or otherwise. 'Judge not, that ye be not judged' right? How I feel is often in complete opposition to the people I grew up with in Mississippi, but I think Tina taught me to think outside the box and that you should never apologize for being your true self.

I think it is important to look for the role models in your life, whether they are conventional mentors such as parents or teachers or crazy and off-the-wall people like Tina. If you pay close attention you will see that we all have folks around us who are living proof that anything is possible. Reach out and ask them for advice. You never have to go it alone.

Tina died a few years ago and although we had drifted apart I feel grateful to have had her in my life. My Paw Paw used to say, 'That Tina is a mess,' but in some ways I think she was the most together of any of us. She showed me that it is OK to speak your mind and go against the grain. I wouldn't be who I am without her.

On the difficult days when I could not evoke my inner Tina, I would lock myself in my room or retreat to the woods next to our trailer. There, nestling between the trees, was my very own sanctuary. A clubhouse which my grandfather had built for me with a linoleum floor, curtains and even a power cable for electricity. I'd work on my journals and listen to Alanis Morissette's album *Jagged Little Pill* on my walkman. I'd turn up 'You Oughta Know' and sing along defiantly to the lyrics.

Tess Holliday's Advice for life #75:
Sing along to music even if you're tone deaf
(...I'm a little tone deaf).

Some days when I felt particularly defeated I'd get stuck into Little Debbie cookies or packets of Cheetos. I felt guilty about sneaking snacks out the kitchen (Mom once got really mad when she found peanut butter and jelly stashed under my bed) but it was a quick fix to fill the void when I was feeling emotional, persecuted or unloved.

Sometimes I wondered if life would be easier if I wasn't around. I didn't want to deal with the bullying any more and I would cry uncontrollably, letting all the sadness out.

Often after a good cry I would feel better and ready to face the world again. I reminded myself I had my mom, my brother and my grandparents. They were the people who loved me and that mattered.

Remembering that I had survived worse situations than this I would walk around the manmade pond on Maw and Paw's land lost in my thoughts or ride my bike up and down the dirt gravel road to our trailer. Being outside in the fresh air and sunshine normally helped me lift my spirits.

* * *

Life at West Jones wasn't all bad. I had a friend called Marie, a petite, olive-skinned girl who was a social misfit like me with braces and, in certain lights, a fetching mustache on her top lip. After school I would go round to her house and act like a fool in front of her parents' video recorder (I know, how retro!). We would dress up in off-the-shoulder shirts and chunky jewelry from the dollar store and film ourselves singing Spice Girls and No Doubt songs. I am eternally grateful that YouTube did not yet exist.

We also performed alto together in our school choir 'Singers' and travelled all over Mississippi singing in competitions. We weren't as cool as show choir – the *Glee*-style big personality performers who could sing and dance – but we nailed the Christmas song 'Carol of the Bells' and the state song of Mississippi.

The show choir kids got to wear sequins while we made do with dowdy, made-to-measure black skirts and tops. We may have been a bunch of nerds but the kids in Singers were nice. A couple of the girls were on the heavier side like me and there was a real feeling of solidarity. As cheesy as it sounds we could get lost in our Singers sessions where we found we could be whoever we wanted to be. Our singing was awesome and no one was judging us for anything else.

I tried not to boast about our achievements too much because I had been taught at church that if God gave you a talent you shouldn't use it to serve yourself. This genuinely terrified me as a child. I had a good singing voice and had a superstitious inkling that if I sang too much I would wake up one day and my voice would be gone.

I'd end up mute like Ariel in *The Little Mermaid* after Ursula took her voice.

Aside from Singers, I loved acting out *Romeo and Juliet* in drama and I would geek out in computer class trying to beat my own super-fast touch-typing record. While I excelled in the classes that sparked my enthusiasm, I was still hindered by my short attention span. I would daydream during the subjects I found boring and rarely did my homework. While Tad brought home glowing report cards, mine were often hit or miss.

As my thirteenth birthday approached in July 1998, Mom decided to throw me a fancy birthday bash. She and Tina set about organizing the party of all parties, with no detail overlooked.

Mom loved to bake so out came all her favorite recipe books and she instructed me to pick which cakes I wanted. I spent ages flicking through the pages, salivating over all the baked treats, trying to choose the ones I wanted. There was a beautiful butterfly cake, another shaped like a caterpillar and a chocolate cake with vanilla icing.

The party venue was a small local hall in Laurel with a kitchen, folding chairs and tables, which could accommodate up to 80 guests. We used it for most of our family functions, including the time my brother almost set it on fire at a family reunion. A budding pyromaniac, he found some matches and headed outside to light some dry grass. Before he knew it the fence had caught fire and the flames were heading for the building. Thankfully Uncle

Don intervened, grabbing an extinguisher and putting out the flames. I'd like to say Tad learnt his lesson but he continued to be obsessed with fire. For a while his favorite adolescent trick was to set a stream of hairspray alight so it blazed like a propane torch. Once he scorched the end of my hair playing with a lighter. He's a liability.

As I approached the momentous milestone of becoming a teenager, I was desperate to overhaul my image. It was my dream to have blonde highlights but up until now I had not been allowed to color my hair. Eventually my pleading worked and Mom agreed I could have highlights.

My hair appointment was the morning of the party. Mom and I arrived bright and early at the suburban home of a hairdresser who saw clients in her house. Sat in her kitchen I felt very grown up as she put a highlighting cap over my head. For the longest time she worked on my hair, pulling small sections through the cap with an instrument that looked like a crochet needle. Next she mixed up a strong smelling concoction and smothered it over the hair protruding from the cap. I sat there excitedly, waiting for the dye to work its magic.

Finally the hairdresser directed me to the sink where she used a detachable showerhead to wash off the remnants of the chemical smelling lotion. Sitting me back on the chair she set to work blow-drying my tresses. I eagerly awaited my big reveal, imagining how beautiful I'd look with my new Jennifer Anniston hair. But as she turned me around to face the mirror I could only gasp. There was not a swishy, blonde lock in sight. My hair was GREY.

It turned out that this woman, masquerading as a hair stylist, spent most of her working days beautifying pensioners. How she butchered my blonde bouffant I will never know.

I sat there seething and struggling not to cry as she cooed over her work.

'Is she colorblind?' I wondered. If only the crochet stick had been close at hand to stab her with.

As is often the case with hair disasters Mom and I reacted politely, staging forced grimaces and left. The moment I got into the car I burst into tears.

'I look like Grandma!' I cried.

'It still looks nice!' Mom insisted. 'Don't let it ruin your day.'

She was being so sympathetic that suddenly I felt bad. Remembering all the love and care she had put into my party I accepted a tissue and made the decision to suck it up.

Arriving at the venue I was amazed at the trouble Mom had gone to. As well as crafting the cakes, she had slaved away baking homemade chocolate chip cookies and had filled bowls full of Doritos and Lays chips. The spread looked incredible. She and Tina had decorated the place beautifully with balloons and banners. There was even a DJ hired from the local radio station. Keep in mind my mom had no money, it was an incredible feat that she pulled it off.

With butterflies in my stomach I waited excitedly for the kids from my school to show up. I had invited my entire class. The party start time came and went with a handful of my relatives arriving, but there was still no one from school. I watched the door, reminding myself that people never show up on time. I ate some chips and chatted to Mom and Tina to kill the time, ignoring the fact that 30 minutes had now gone by.

After an hour, Brooke and Marie bustled in and I tried to stay hopeful that any minute now more kids from school would burst through the doors. The DJ kept the music pumping and I swayed along to 'Ghetto Supastar' and 'Boom Shake the Room', my eyes constantly flitting to the hall entrance.

Finally, after two hours, I realized no one else was showing up. When Mom smiled sympathetically my eyes filled with tears. As she gave me a hug I looked around the hall again at her handiwork. She and Tina had poured so much love and hard work into my party. Wiping my eyes I decided to make the most of it.

I asked the DJ to play 'Walk like an Egyptian' and the 'Macarena' and danced and laughed with my friends. The fact that only two friends had turned up was soul-crushing but I reminded myself to appreciate the people who were here.

'Fuck 'em!' Tina remarked, planting a kiss on my forehead. She was right and once again I embraced her potty-mouthed life mantra.

Tess Holliday's Advice for life #77:
Even if no one is there to join in,
dance to the beat of your own drum.

My birthday debacle was not the last time life kicked me in the vagina. I'd just sorted out my granny chic highlights when my hormones went insane and I got acne. Thanks world!

I was super paranoid about my pimples and tried to mask my skin by caking on layer upon layer of make-up. I was not very good at applying foundation so most of the time I had a fetching orange face and a mismatched neck. This was at a time before teenage girls could gather tips from *YouTube* make-up tutorials, but luckily Mom came to my rescue. She presented me with a book by make-up artist Kevyn Aucoin and I read it from cover to cover. It became my bible. This was definitely the point where my love of make-up began.

Mom's efforts to improve my life were continuous. After catching me crying about the acne that plagued my forehead, cheeks and chin she raced to the rescue. 'We'll try tanning beds,' she announced. In the 1990s everyone down south fried their skin with artificial rays, blissfully unaware of just how dangerous it was to their health. To the contrary, tanned skin was believed to help you look slimmer, clear up acne and alleviate a bunch of other ailments. Mom already swore by tanning beds to ease the pain in her neck from the imbedded bullet fragments. The ultraviolet light helped a lot with the inflammation and she loved the feeling of heat on her skin.

As much as I wanted good skin I never took to tanning beds the way Mom did. I hated the feeling of lying on the sweaty plastic and getting my body burnt. The sessions made me sticky and uncomfortable and I didn't care at all for the 'burnt sugar' aroma that lingered after a skin frying session. My last ever session was in someone's trailer with a crappy neon sign outside.

'You go first!' Mom instructed, ushering me into a makeshift booth. But although I stripped naked I just could not bring myself to go under the penetrating blue light. Instead I stood with my back to the rays, shuffling on my feet for 15 minutes until my slot was up.

When I redressed and exited the booth I was faced by Mom. She looked mad.

'I saw your feet under the door,' she fumed. 'I'm not paying for any more sessions if you're going to waste it.' I felt slightly guilty but happy with the outcome.

Nowadays sunbeds are considered to be even more harmful than going in the sun and my mom no longer uses them after she got a melanoma. Thankfully the cancer was contained and didn't spread but it was the wake-up call she needed to give up the sunbeds for good.

When I go home to the South I am always amazed by the number of tanning salons I still see. I don't know why anyone would want to risk dying from cancer for the sake of getting a tan. It's far better to be pale, interesting ... and living!

I still suffer from the occasional acne break out but rather than bake my face under a sun lamp I know to nurture my skin and treat it with respect.

As a model I get asked a lot for skincare tips and I always say that the best things you can do are eat a healthy, balanced diet and drink lots of water. My other beauty rules are to apply SPF to your face, neck and décolletage and to avoid touching or picking at your blemishes. That just spreads bacteria and makes the area worse. I also advise cleaning your make-up brushes once a week with brush cleaner or a good anti-bacterial soap plus giving your skin a break from make-up once or twice a week.

My last tip is to get some SLEEP! As the exhausted mother of a baby who is seemingly allergic to sleep I cannot emphasize enough how awesome a good night's rest is. If you have the luxury of uninterrupted sleep then snooze while you can. Sleep is so healing for your body, mind and soul. I miss it!

* * *

Almost a year after he destroyed my swim team dreams my father tried a different, more sensitive tactic to encourage me to lose weight. He had recently remarried, tying the knot with a woman called Lisa who was at least five years younger than Dad and loved Scooby-Doo, coca cola slushies and Ozzy Osbourne. Lisa seemed like a good influence on Dad and I liked her a lot. She was always very motherly to me, taking me to the movies or on shopping trips to the mall. When she joined Weight Watchers, Dad offered to pay for me to do it too. They bought me Weight Watchers approved frozen meals and were surprisingly supportive.

As a US size 16 teenager I did aspire to be thinner. Most of the feedback I was getting was that it was wrong to be fat and I did wonder if losing weight would make me happy or more popular.

I followed the diet for a couple of weeks but to be honest my heart wasn't in it. I didn't like the way it took the fun out of food for me. Part of the joy of eating is being able to make choices on the fly, to decide what you're in the mood for and to savor the taste. I didn't like having to count, measure and weigh my food each time I ate. It felt regimented and didn't sit right with me. While I appreciated all my father and his girlfriend were trying to do, I wasn't interested in counting every-thing I ate.

Tess Holliday's Advice for Life #81: You're allowed to enjoy food.

Now when I hear of carb-dodging celebrities who get their personal assistants to phone ahead to restaurants to order low-calorie meals I feel sorry for them. Yes, they may have so-called 'perfect' beach bodies but imagine living your life like that?

Tess Holliday's Advice for Life #88:
All you need for a beach body is to take your
body to the beach. People of all shapes and sizes
are allowed to enjoy their bodies outdoors.

While I aspired to lose weight, not being able to eat what I wanted made me miserable. I was yet to embark on my path to self-love and embracing my body exactly as it is, but that was the first and last time I tried to crash diet.

That summer I felt like my relationship with my father improved. There was no doubt Lisa was a good influence on him.

'I was put on this earth to put up with your dad,' she often told me while shaking her head. 'No one else would!'

When Dad was in good spirits he could be a lot of fun. He loved to sing Bee Gees songs in an earsplitting falsetto in public to embarrass us, or stick out his leg in a comedic fashion while bowling.

'It makes my aim better,' he claimed with a wink.

But eventually his temper always got the better of him and everything could be ruined in a heartbeat.

When he lost his shit he could be vicious and there was no such thing as stooping too low. During one heated argument, he even announced that I had a sister the same age who lived in Alabama. I thought it was another tall tale intended to hurt me until Mom confirmed it. She said that she'd always heard rumors that Dad had got someone else pregnant around the time she was having me.

That summer when Dad announced he was taking Tad and me to Disney World we almost shat out pants with excitement. Even though I had reached my teens I still loved Disney movies, especially *The Little Mermaid* and *Beauty and the Beast*. A visit to Disney World was up there at the top of my 'dreams come true' list. In the weeks leading up to the trip I could think of nothing else. I would get to see the Cinderella Castle in The Magic Kingdom and have my photo taken with all the different Disney characters!

We piled into the car at the crack of dawn to make the long drive from Alabama to Orlando, Florida. After eight hours on the road we pulled into the parking lot of our budget hotel, everyone cranky and tired. As Dad and Tad climbed out the car, I was busy picking up the books, candy, Barbies and various other treasures I had scattered all over the backseat.

'We'll see you up there,' Dad said, pulling the suitcases out of the car. He handed me the keys and told me to lock the car door.

After cramming everything into my backpack I jumped out the car and rushed up the steps to our room. 'I wonder if you can see the castle from the window?' I thought.

When I arrived in the room I saw Dad stood by the window. He was looking down at the parking lot and had a look of thunder on his face.

'Ryann!' he shouted. 'You left the car door open.' Quick as a flash he lunged towards me and slapped me.

'Do you want someone to steal our stuff?' he screamed. Then he took off his belt and began to beat me on my arms and legs. I tried to back away from him but he was relentless. Sobbing, I ran into the bathroom and locked the door. I sunk to the floor with my legs to my chest. I was trembling all over. He had beaten me before but never with this much ferocity.

After about half an hour I unlocked the door and tentatively peered into the room. I was relieved to see my father's face was calmer.

'Sorry,' he mumbled. 'But you shouldn't have left the car door open.'

While he was feeling repentant the blame clearly went to me for behaving in a way that 'made him do it'.

Every time Dad lashed out at me a little bit inside me died. It made me sad, depressed and nervous about the world. I never told my mom what happened on that trip. I didn't want to upset her or make the situation worse.

I get that it is hard being a parent. No one pushes your buttons like your kids and even the best of us get mad and lose it. But as an adult you have to stop yourself and think about what you are doing. Last year history repeated itself when my older son ignored my request to stay in the car and followed us into the store, leaving the engine running and my purse on the seat. I was pretty pissed off but I didn't beat the shit out of him!

When Bowie wakes multiple times a night screaming and I feel physically sick from exhaustion, parenting feels like a thankless task and a little like torture. I am often reduced to tears, I want to scream, I want to shout, I want to ask God, Buddha, Beyoncé – all the main deities – what I did to deserve this frustration, but would I physically harm my child? Never.

When Dad attacked me at Disney World I think that was the beginning of my slow retreat away from him. It tugged at my heartstrings for a long time but eventually, in my late twenties, I cut him out my life for good. Maybe it was harsh but I believe that if someone isn't treating you the way you deserve to be treated they don't deserve to be part of your life. Family or not, they have to earn a seat at my table.

Tess Holliday's Advice for Life #94:
Never feel guilty for cutting a toxic
family member out of your life.

Chapter 4

Too Fat, Too Short

I was 15 when I first tried to break into the plus size model industry. While some mothers might be dismissive of their size 16 daughter dreaming of modeling fame, my mom actively encouraged me.

'You could do it!' she said. 'I think you're beautiful.'

Despite my confidence suffering a devastating blow from the bullying at school, I did know I was photogenic at least. People often commented on how nice I looked in pictures and ever since Mom had bought MY bible – the gospel according to Kevyn Aucoin – my make-up efforts had improved greatly. Yes, my ass and thighs were considerably bigger than Heidi Klum's and Naomi Campbell's combined, but Mom had always drummed it into me that anything was possible. It's hard to disagree with advice like that from someone who's been shot executioner style and fought her way back … She's not quite 50 Cent, but she's at least a nickel. While I still hadn't got to a point where I was able to fully love myself, my dreams were big and Mom had taught me to be determined.

My mom took me shopping at Lane Bryant and I found myself staring at the curvy models in their advertising campaigns, wondering if I could be like them. These women seemed so comfortable in their own skin; I wanted to achieve that too.

Tess Holliday's Advice for Life #97:
Everyone deserves to see themselves
represented in the media. Representation
can be incredibly empowering!

I think Mom understood that I needed some direction, or something to strive for to get me through the victimization I was facing at school. Plus my defensive habit of shutting down, tuning out and retreating into myself really wasn't helping my grades. Being 'away with the fairies' meant that I rarely applied myself and I finished eighth grade having failed everything apart from art, drama, computing and health class. Just when I thought things couldn't get any worse I was held down a year to repeat the grade. Go me!

Of course, Tad was less than impressed to have his 'stupid sister' in his school year, but luckily for him we were in different classes because of our grades. As always, he breezed through school life with enviable ease as a member of the 'popular gang'. I would watch with disgust as the semi-popular kids attempted to suck up to Tad while turning up their noses at me, his weirdo sister.

It would have been nice of Tad to throw me a lifeline but he never did. Regrettably our relationship as siblings was never that close. Even now, as adults, it sometimes feels like we are a world apart from each other.

With Mom worried sick about my floundering self-esteem and low moods she immediately embraced my enthusiasm for a plus model casting show in Atlanta I'd heard about on the radio. Part of the rather expensive ticket was a chance to walk a 'runway' in front of industry professionals from *bona fide* modeling and talent agencies. They would give you feedback and possibly your big break into modeling! Given that we lived 350 miles away from Atlanta it was a big ask but Mom agreed to talk to my stepdad, Bill, about it. I don't want to know what she had to do in return, but Bill agreed to buy tickets and I was one step closer to my modeling dream.

Before we headed to the show I needed photos for my 'modeling portfolio' so Mom hired a local portrait photographer. I picked my make-up carefully, using black and white eyeliner, and dressed in black capri pants and a silver shirt with ruched sleeves unbuttoned over a white tank top. I completed my look with open-toed cowhide clogs. Very high fashion. My hair was short and flipped out on the sides. I was very pleased with my look but in reality I looked more like a 40-year-old bankteller from the Midwest than an aspiring model.

At the shoot, I sat on a wooden stool looking awkward – I had no clue how to pose.

'Sit up straight,' the photographer instructed. 'Now lower your head slightly and look up at me.'

Next I sat on the ground with my legs out. I had my back to the photographer and was looking over my shoulder and smiling. In hindsight the poses were pretty weird. It was not a sophisticated shoot. But I had my 'professional' shots so I was happy.

The day before the show, Mom, Bill and I set off to Atlanta in the family mini-van. My brother, who was not at all interested in my lame modeling aspirations, stayed at home with our grandparents. It took us eight hours to get to Atlanta and we arrived by early evening. Bill had booked us into the hotel where the event was being held. It was so fancy with a huge suite for Mom and Bill and a separate room for me. Looking back I don't know how they afforded it.

On the morning of the show I awoke early with butterflies in my tummy and spent ages getting ready. I decided to keep my outfit simple, opting for jeans, a blue V neck t-shirt and natural make-up.

The show was held in a huge event space at the hotel with multiple symposiums. The halls were packed out and buzzing with excited teenage girls who had clearly spent months planning their outfits. Many were wearing double denim, accessorized with studded belts, choker necklaces and trucker-style baseball caps. I suddenly felt like my outfit was very plain in comparison. It reminded me of how I felt at school, the weird girl with thrift store clothes. I watched in awe as these wannabe fashionistas flitted from exhibit to exhibit reapplying frosted lip gloss with unwavering teenage attitude. Undeterred, I spent the morning browsing the endless booths selling clothes and beauty products. Every so often I would pause to look up at a stage presenting hair and make-up tutorials or catwalk walking lessons.

Exercise classes were included in the ticket so Mom and I signed up for an hour-long introduction to yoga, which made me feel so worldly and enlightened. No one was doing yoga in Mississippi at the time so when I got home I made sure I smugly told anyone who would listen about it.

My time slot to walk the catwalk and meet the judges was in the early afternoon and as my big moment approached I started to feel slightly less zen. My stomach churned with nervous excitement and I had to go to the toilet several times.

When the time came, I congregated with the other hopefuls backstage, closing my eyes and trying to breathe slowly to calm myself, just like I'd learnt in yoga. When I opened my eyes again I was surprised to see a couple of girls looking at me. One whispered to the other and they started giggling. I had a bad feeling I was the source of their amusement. They were both tall and at least two dress sizes smaller than me. Looking around it suddenly occurred to me that all the girls in my group were like this. Everyone was at least five feet eight in height and a size 12 at the most. Everyone but me. At five feet three and a size 16 I was considerably bigger and shorter.

For a moment I felt very self-conscious and out of place, but then I started to get annoyed. 'This is my dream too,' I thought. 'I'll try out to be a model if I damn well want to.'

My thoughts were interrupted by the first girl being summoned to walk the runway.

One by one other girls in our group were called out and then suddenly it was my turn.

My heart pounded as I stepped foot on to the runway and looked out to a sea of faces. There must have been 500 people watching, 50 of whom I knew worked for model and booking agencies. I saw Mom waving and smiling and I tried not to focus on anyone else.

Praying that I would not trip I did my best to sway down the catwalk in time to the pumping music. At the end of the runway I stopped and placed my hand on my hip like I'd seen on fashion documentaries. I am sure I looked ridiculous but I was proud of myself for having the guts to do it (no pun intended).

With the runway walks over there was a feeling of exhilaration backstage. I joined the other girls as they laughed and chatted excitedly waiting for the callbacks. We'd been told that if an industry professional saw potential we would be handed a sheet of paper.

The runner arrived with a wad of papers and began to hand them out.

I watched in trepidation as the two giggling girls received a handful each. Most of the girls were getting a stack of papers. 'Oh God,' I thought. 'What if I don't get anything?'

'Ryann?' the runner asked. I stepped forward and he thrust a single sheet of paper into my now clammy palms. I gripped the sheet, my chest swelling with pride. Meeting Mom outside I jumped up and down with happiness.

'I have a callback from a booking agency!' I told her proudly.

Ten minutes later I stood feeling nervous as a tall, thin man in his late twenties looked me up and down.

'Here's my portfolio,' I said, handing him the black scrapbook that had my photos in. He studied it in a disinterested manner for a matter of seconds. Then he handed it back.

'You're not tall enough and you're too big,' he said. 'You might be able to work but the best would be catalogue work.'

I was winded by his bluntness and quickly sloped back to Mom.

'What did he say?' she asked seeing my dejected face.

I repeated the agent's words while trying not to cry.

'Well he obviously saw your potential,' Mom told me, putting her arms around me.

I nodded and swallowed down the feeling of disappointment. Perhaps it was time to put my dream of being a model on the back burner, but I wasn't about to give up for good.

* * *

Back in Laurel I shoved my 'portfolio' into a drawer and flopped down on my bed with my Kevyn Aucoin book. Maybe my modeling career was on hold for now but I could still work in the industry as a make-up artist. So I continued to spend hours practicing different looks with make-up Mom had got me from the Avon catalogue. I felt like my skills were improving and I was getting the best kind of positive feedback ... guys at school were taking an interest in me.

Up until now my kissing experience consisted of smooching my New Kids on the Block wall posters and the time I got into trouble age five because a boy kissed me on the swing set. Marie and I had been speculating for months about what it would be like to kiss someone 'with tongues' when suddenly I found out. Ryan, a boy I liked from school, made an attempt to French kiss me.

Beforehand I had wanted to kiss Ryan so bad. He was tall, blonde and skinny with spikey hair and blue eyes and I had the biggest crush on him. I'd been passing him notes in school for a while but assumed he wasn't in to me because my fellow classmates never missed an opportunity to remind me I was fat and not at all cool. But then one day Ryan invited me over to his house after school. I almost fainted on the spot. This was my big chance! We went up to his bedroom and he made his move. I was beside myself with breathy anticipation.

As he went in for the big moment I closed my eyes and pouted my lips. Perhaps my poster kissing practice had been for nothing, because this didn't feel at all like I thought it would. And why was my nose wet? My nose was IN HIS MOUTH. It was not the dreamy moment I had been waiting for. I quickly recoiled and wiped my face. Oh Ryan! I don't know where he is now, but I hope he's out there licking all the nostrils he can. I continued to have a crush on him despite that horrible kiss – until I fell for a boy in my church youth group.

Tess Holliday's Advice for Life #101:
Life's too short for shitty kisses. Same goes for
shitty sex. Communicate what it is you want
and if they don't give it to you ... NEXT!

Religion was compulsory in our home with Mom insisting we go to the First Baptist Church of Shady Grove every Wednesday and twice on Sunday. Before the evening service on Wednesdays, Tad and I would attend youth group. It was led by a dorky but nice youth minister called Jonathan who was tall with black hair and blue eyes. He was in his mid-twenties and had a fiancée called Mandy who was also very active in the church. The youth group mainly consisted of lessons from the Bible and then we would go over the hymns for the main church service.

I went to church because Mom wanted me to, but the older I got the more I struggled with some of the interpretations of God's message. Our church preached about 'loving your neighbor' but largely seemed to ignore the impoverished members of the black minority of the town. The completely backwards view was that 'kind should stay with kind' and I would learn later that interracial dating was more than frowned upon.

I also could not understand how suffering was part of God's plan especially when people die or get cancer. The explanations 'God doesn't give you more than you can handle' or 'God just needed another angel' were hard to accept. Why would it ever be 'in God's plan' for a child to die from cancer?

Sometimes I wondered if I was being lied to but then I'd feel guilty for going against what my family believed. Mom was adamant she was alive because of 'God's plan' but in my mind being told that everything had already been pre-decided for me freaked me out.

'I feel like life is basically a board game,' I confided to Mom. 'We're the pawns being moved around without any say.'

'You have control but God is there to help you decide between right and wrong,' Mom tried to reason, but I still could not shake the feeling that I had to rely on an invisible man in the sky to decide my fate. I hated being told to pray when times were hard.

Why couldn't we be more proactive and make a change through our own actions?

Jonathan, to his credit, knew that Tad and I, as well as some of the other kids, were there reluctantly at our parents' request and would do his best to be empathetic.

'I used to have a drug problem,' he'd joke. 'My parents DRUG me to church every Sunday and DRUG me home again.'

But youth group wasn't without its perks. Yes, there was a lot of talk about Jesus but also: CUTE BOYS AND SNACKS! We were all normal teenagers and everyone was crushing on each other. We got to go on some fun trips including church youth camps in Missouri, Texas and Tennessee. The highlight of the camps for me were the performers they would bring in, some of whom were actually pretty good. There is one who stands out in my memory – his name omitted to avoid the wrath of the church. He was the most flamboyant man my little Southern heart had ever come across. Apparently he is straight, but picture a young Alan Thicke crossed with Liberace, complete with flamenco attire and buff spandex clad male backup dancers. Draw your own conclusions. He was, in a word, fabulous. A moment of satin and sequins in a sea of camouflage cargo shorts.

I liked going to different places without my parents around – especially when I could make eyes at Brad, a boy I'd had my eye on for a while.

Spookily Brad and I had been born on the same day, at the same time in 1985 at South Central Regional Medical Center. How about that for written in the stars? At five feet three, he was a good two inches shorter than me but he had olive skin, luscious dark, curly hair and more than a passing resemblance to the brooding movie star John Cusack. He also had acne and dressed like a weirdo in ridiculous wide-legged JNCO pants with studded belts and goth shirts, which sounds like a train-wreck but I found it all endearing.

Brad's life had not been easy either. His father had been killed by a drunk driver and his mother was addicted to drugs and unable to care for him. We bonded over our shared experiences of being oddballs and having a hard family life. He lived with his grandmother in a house across the street from our church. Romance blossomed as we exchanged eye rolls at Jonathan's lame jokes and passed notes to each other at school. I was pretty sure he was my soulmate.

After weeks of flirting Brad finally said the words I wanted to hear: 'Do you want to be my girlfriend?'

For a while we were the epitome of a sweet, teenage romance. We would hang out at each other's houses smooching and play fighting on the couch. We would go to the movies together and make out in the dark and discreetly brush fingertips as we sat next to each other at church.

At school I would often discover love letters from Brad in my locker. He would also make cute, handmade cards out of construction paper or doodles of us together and sneak them into my book bag. He was always telling me I was pretty or that he loved me and wanted to marry me. I was head over heels in love with him too and smiled every time I thought about him.

There was no doubt my relationship with Brad gave me a real confidence boost. For so long I'd felt like a freak at school but suddenly I didn't care what anyone had to say about my size or appearance. It gave me a confirmation that what I thought was true: that bodies of all shapes and sizes could be beautiful. I didn't need to be like everyone else to bag a boyfriend. Life was looking up.

Around this time I got my first job at Southern Styles – a hair, nail and tanning salon in a local shopping center. It was a fairly easy job. I would go after school, answer the phone, fold the towels and make sure the customers were OK. When the tanning customers were done with their 30-minute appointment I would wipe down the sunbeds. During the quiet spells I could amuse myself as I pleased and sometimes Brad or one of my girlfriends would come by and we'd sit on the couch and watch trash TV.

When I wasn't working or seeing Brad I would hang out with Marie gossiping in our bedrooms and listening to our favorite band, Incubus. I had a short-lived friendship with a girl named Bridget, with whom I'd skipped school for shits and giggles. I'd like to say we planned an epic adventure on a par with *Ferris Bueller's Day Off* but we didn't really think it through. After getting take-out from our favorite burger place, PDI's, we headed back to Bridget's house and made a whole lot of noise in the room next to where her mother was sleeping off her Walmart night shift. She awoke in a fury and I was quickly sent home and my AWOL adventure reported back. Mom was mad as hell and punished me by taking away my prized ticket to see Incubus on tour. That burger was so not worth it and I never skipped school again.

Tess Holliday's Advice for Life #113: Don't skip school at your parents' co-worker's house. They will find out. Duh.

Growing up in Mississippi, I only really ever hung out with kids who had been in the South all their lives, so when a petite French chick appeared in my speech and debate class I was intrigued. I immediately befriended Adéline, a foreign exchange student, and pumped her for information about life in Europe. Adéline could speak little English but was very expressive using her face and hands to add to whatever she was trying to say. I remember thinking how shitty it must have been to find out she was going to America to study and then being sent to Mississippi, but she loved it. She said she liked how convenient everything was compared to France where 'fast' food was just not an option. She was obsessed with Southern dishes and for a tiny person she could polish off an impressive-sized portion of fried chicken and grits. Even as a sheltered girl from the South I understood the absurdity of this given that the French are world-renowned for their cuisine.

Over the eight months of her exchange, Adéline and I became close and she would hang out at my house several times a week. One such evening after school I decided to show her one of my all-time favorite movies, *Deuce Bigalow: Male Gigolo*. It was clear that Adéline did not understand all the scenes so I did my best to translate – paying special attention to the raunchy bits. Thankfully Adéline thought it was hysterical and it quickly became her favorite film too.

After that I decided my friend needed to be introduced to all my favorite things and before long she was singing along to Ludacris songs pouting out lines about 'homies', which actually sounded like 'omies' in her adorable French accent. Observing all this, Mom expressed concern for Adéline, who she believed was super-vulnerable to being led astray being so far away from home.

'I feel so sad that she doesn't understand our language,' she said. 'Should you be teaching her stuff like that?'

'She calls me Porky,' I retorted, letting my Mom know her affectionate nickname for me, 'so I think she understands me just fine.'

She was not amused.

Mom had recently become more vocal about how it was 'our responsibility' to tell people about God. I was alarmed to realize she had Adéline in her sights.

'You need to ask Adéline if she believes in Jesus,' she told me. 'It is your job to make sure she is going to heaven.'

Her request made me uncomfortable. She knew I was beginning to question the teachings of the church. I had grown up hearing how disbelievers had a one-way ticket to hell and it was hard to fathom. So if you've never heard of God, you'll go to heaven, but if you decide you don't believe in him you'll go to hell? Even my hormone-addled, teenage brain couldn't make sense of that. I decided to leave the God talk out of my time with Adéline and introduce her to chili cheese fries and BLTs instead. My Grandpa's fried okra? Now that's a religious experience! Praise Crisco I've seen the light!

* * *

A few months into our relationship Brad and I got into a big fight.

I don't remember what it was about but I was shocked when he called me a bitch. He had never lashed out at me before and his words hurt me. I spent the next day moping in class and wondering if my relationship was doomed. But when school was over for the day I found Brad waiting outside for me. He was holding up a posterboard.

'I'm sorry,' it read.

Then he shuffled another in front of it: 'Please forgive me.'

Then a third: 'I love you!'

At the time I thought it was so romantic and it was *way* before the film *Love Actually* came out. In the film, Andrew Lincoln's character turns up with those cards, just like Brad did, silently professing his undying love for Keira Knightley. How lovely right? Oh wait, it's completely insane. I mean, SHE'S MARRIED and her HUBAND IS

HOME, which is awkward enough for her and a good reason NOT TO SHOW UP ON HER DOORSTEP, but the fact that it was all premeditated, showing up silently with those ready-made cards pretending to be a caroler is FIFTY SHADES OF FUCKED UP. Not romantic, buddy – creepy. Hella creepy. I was young and inexperienced, and so, much like Keira Knightley's character, I accepted Brad's grand gesture of love.

Growing up in the Bible belt, I knew that the popular belief was that sex before marriage was a sin. You were supposed to stay pure for your wedding night. This was the message clearly preached by Jonathan in youth group, yet ignored by Brad, who, five months into our relationship, began to put the moves on me.

At 15 I did not know a lot about sex. People from Laurel (and Mississippi in general) were very conservative and sex education classes in school were non-existent. The limited information I had about 'doing it' had been gleaned from giggling friends at school and a book my mom had read to me about how people 'fall in love, get married and then have sex'.

Then there was Tina who was always 'doing it' with various boyfriends and would sometimes greet me with the question, 'Have you flicked the bean today?' leaving Mom audibly gasping in shock, and me blushing but elated at the openness she brought to my life. Once, when I was at her trailer, she pulled out a box of sex toys from under the bed.

'This is pinky!' she yelled, waggling a large pink vibrator. She was a true 'sex positive' feminist who didn't care who knew about her sex life and would cuss out anyone who disagreed with how she lived her life. But she was the exception to the rule, and what an oppressive rule it was. However, regardless of whether the good town-folk of Laurel thought it was ungodly or not, there was a more pressing concern. We were both 15 and in no way ready to have sex.

It was not uncommon for our kissing sessions to get quite handsy and heated, but whenever I pulled back Brad would get sulky.

'I thought you loved me,' he said.

Ouch. It was a below the belt tactic to get well, below the belt. I didn't know what to do. I did love Brad but did that mean I had to put out? While I wanted to be with him, I also felt things were moving too fast. I still had pangs of guilt about the hand job I'd given him under a blanket at the back of the church bus while my mom and my cousin Randy sat up front. (Sorry Mom!) Whenever Brad's hands veered south to wrestle with my panties I would immediately tense up. In those moments I felt trepidation, not passion – an entirely normal reaction for a 15-year-old girl being pressured into having sex before she is ready. But every time Brad acted rejected, I also felt bad and worried for making him feel frustrated. What if he dumped me?

Like many lustful teenage boys, Brad lacked the emotional maturity to be gentlemanly in this situation. He could not take no for an answer. His advances happened again and again. We'd start making out, his hands would wander and then he'd get shitty when I didn't want to take it any further.

Eventually he wore me down and my momentous metamorphosis into womanhood occurred in Brad's open-plan loft bedroom as his grandmother shuffled around below.

It was all super awkward as I grappled, clueless, with the condom and Brad had to put it on himself. I lay there tensely, with one eye on the door, as he got on top of me and awkwardly pushed inside me. I waited for the pain. Would I feel my hymen break? Everyone said you bled and stuff the first time. But there was none of that.

As Brad put his full weight on me, I wasn't even sure he had it in. There was some fumbling and face pulling then he lay on my chest, hot breath on my shoulder. He panted rapidly and I assumed it was over.

The memory of my first time still bums me out. I should not have been pressured to have sex before I felt ready. I was too young and, if I hadn't met him, I probably wouldn't have lost my virginity for a long time.

Sex with Brad didn't really get any better after the first time. He would quickly climax and that would be it. I knew nothing about female orgasms and I was unaware that I should be enjoying myself too.

I cringe when I think about the places we did it. On top of a pile of dirty laundry on the bathroom floor?

Yeah, we went there … Why? Because I was scared if I said no I would be alone again. Sadly my motivation to do it came from a place of insecurity. I was not having sex for myself, I was having sex for Brad, catering for his teenage libido and lust in an attempt to hold on to him. Big fucking surprise, it didn't work.

It took me a long time to realize that my worth didn't need to be validated by being wanted by a man … or anyone for that means. We have been told for too long that beauty is tied to someone wanting you, but that's not the case.

However, I also don't think it's entirely true that you have to fully love yourself before you can love someone else – a lot of us will spend a lifetime unlearning the reasons we have been taught not to love ourselves, and that's okay. What's important is that you don't lose sight of the fact that EVERY person is worthy of love and understanding. Have sex with everyone, have sex with no one, have sex with one person your whole life – those choices should come from a place of respect and be YOUR choice. I've slut-shamed women in the past, and if you're one of the people who have felt the cruel sting of that barb I am truly sorry. You live and learn; it wasn't until I was in a loving relationship that my partner could start to help me unpack the ways in which I was externalizing my (mostly Christian) shame around sex.

Never let someone rush or pressure you into having sex. There's no shame in saying NO. Never let someone verbally abuse you or put you down in a relationship, you deserve BETTER. Never compromise who you are to make yourself seem more appealing to someone else. It's just not worth it, THEY aren't worth it.

Chapter 5:

Home of 'The Big One'

I can exactly pinpoint the moment my relationship began to go downhill – it was the day Brad's grandmother died of a heart attack.

That morning Brad called me freaking out. He had been woken by his grandmother's alarm going off. He'd assumed she'd overslept or was in a different part of the house, but when he went into her room there she was, dead on the floor. Hearing his heartbreak over the phone made me feel helpless. I didn't really know what to say to him. I offered to go to his house but he declined.

'I need some space,' he said.

I was hurt but I tried to understand. I had a funny feeling – was Brad pushing me away?

For the next few weeks I tried to support Brad, but his grief was impenetrable. It was understandable. His grandmother was the one adult he felt he could rely on and without her he felt very alone. He continued to live in the house with his uncle but their relationship was not a close one. Now he was fending for himself. I tried to think about how I would feel if my mom had died.

But the more I tried to comfort him the more irritating he seemed to find me. His sense of hopelessness and loss manifested itself in anger as he lashed out at the person closest to him – that was me. So for the next few months I felt like I couldn't do anything right.

Suddenly, being with Brad was like hanging out with my dad. The slightest thing I said could be taken the wrong way and he would snap at me with contempt. I'd crack a joke and he'd tell me angrily I wasn't funny. I'd try to compliment him and somehow he'd take it as an insult. He would break up with me all the time, then express remorse. It was exhausting.

No one had told me that teenage romances are often fragile by nature. When you fall hard into a love affair underpinned with raging hormones and emotional immaturity it can take very little to throw it off kilter. But in our case our relationship was being derailed by something huge. I could feel Brad slipping away from me and it was awful – especially as I had given him my virginity.

I tried to convince myself that sharing our first time meant something and would be the glue to hold us together, but as Brad began to distance himself from me panic set in.

I had invested everything, hoping for a future with my first love but I wasn't sure if he even liked me much any more. To the contrary, he seemed determined to reject everything from his old life.

Maybe it was an act of self-preservation because his past was so painful, but week by week a brooding Brad began to reinvent himself. He started wearing jeans that actually fitted him and collared shirts. He cut his hair so it was short at the sides but curly on the top like the dreamy early 2000s Justin Timberlake. Then his doctor prescribed acne medicine and his skin cleared up. Brad had always played guitar but suddenly he joined a band and began to hang out with some older kids from our school. This new crew listened to punk and saw themselves as rebellious and cool. Whenever I hung out with them I felt uncomfortable – especially if Susie was around. Susie isn't her real name, but I'm not about to give that bitch the satisfaction of getting her name dropped in my book. Sorry 'bout it.

Susie, who was two school years above me and one above Brad, had positioned herself as the queen bee of the gang and scathing put-downs flew off her tongue. I'd always had a self-deprecating sense of humor and the ability to laugh at myself but whenever I spent time with Brad's new gang I felt like the designated idiot of the group.

I cringe when I remember walking up to Brad and his friends discussing the new Blink 182 album, which was cleverly titled *Take Off Your Pants and Jacket*. They all seemed to find this hilarious.

'I don't get it,' I said, failing to spot the obvious pun about masturbation.

'Oh my God Ryann, take off your pants and JACK IT,' Brad explained in a condescending tone. While some guys might find such wide-eyed innocence endearing, I was just annoying.

A few days later, as we were lying in bed, he hit me with a cruel blow: 'You know, if your stomach gets bigger than your boobs I am leaving you,' he told me coldly.

'What?' I replied, sitting up in shock. His words made my heart sink. He had never had a problem with my body before. In fact, he'd told me I was beautiful. Why now? It made me feel worthless, self-conscious and a bunch of other shit.

In hindsight, I wish I had told him to go fuck himself and hauled my lovely soft belly and big fat ass out of there, but I was still yearning for the days when Brad had been nice to me. I get that he was just being cruel because of the pain of losing his grandmother, but instead of holding him accountable I held on to the hope that things would get better. Maybe soon Brad would stop being angry with the world and, in turn, less angry with me?

Tess Holliday's Advice For Life #122:
If a partner tells you to lose weight,
lose them instead.

While I waited for this personality transplant to kick into action, Brad's man makeover and moody James Dean routine was having an effect on the female population of the school. And of course, I hated it. As I followed him around I began to see girls doing double takes in the hallways. I started to feel insecure. I was fat with untamed eyebrows and wore a necklace that said 'brat'. Was Brad leaving me behind?

Now that my boyfriend seemed to find me so un-appealing I was spending more and more time with Adéline. She was due to return to France before long – something I could barely think about – so I decided my parting gift would be to teach her to drive.

* cue AC/DC's 'Highway to Hell'*

In Mississippi you could get your learner's permit at 15 and I had been honing my skills in Driver's Ed class. Stoked at the idea of not having to drive me everywhere, Mom talked my dad into buying me a '92 Mercury Sable car. It was a rust bucket with no air conditioning and peeling paint but it had a CD player so really, what else mattered? Technically, I hadn't passed my driving test, so I was supposed to have a licensed driver in the car with me at all times, but that didn't stop me picking up Adéline and driving her to the parking lot of the Winn Dixie grocery store. There I coaxed her into the driving seat and attempted to teach her everything I knew, which, consid-ering the language barrier, was trickier than catching a muddy pig. Thankfully Adéline was a quick learner and located the brake before she could rear-end a parked car.

Adéline and I are still friends, she still calls me Porky and we still laugh about that year. As far as I know her eternal soul is doing OK.

Not long after Adéline returned to France I crashed my Sable driving too fast around a corner. Mom had warned me to slow down because there was new gravel on the road near our house but naturally I hadn't listened. When I hit the brakes too hard I began to skid, hitting a bridge head on. The car spun around and the back end hit too. I wasn't hurt, but it definitely scared the daylights out of me. I got out the car and ran over to my neighbor's house for help. It was only after I had walked through their home to call my mom, bawling my eyes out that I looked down at my beloved cowhide clogs which were covered in hot tar and gravel. Just my luck! In my panic I'd smeared a murky, sticky trail over my neighbor's carpet. I offered to pay but being kind they flat out refused. Now whenever I drive past their house in Laurel I always feel bad about destroying their carpet.

Well, after that my parents weren't happy. With Lisa and Dad recently becoming new parents to a baby boy they named Gabriel my timing was terrible. Begrudgingly my dad found the cash for a teal-colored 1992 Mazda Protégé.

When I arrived in Alabama Dad explained that my new Mazda was a stick shift. I'd only ever driven automatics. Before I went anywhere I would need to learn how to work the clutch and the handbrake. Dad's home was on top of a hill so the pressure was considerable.

'If you can get the car off the slope without wrecking my house, garage or boat, it's yours,' he laughed.

I was terrified but Dad kept his cool, calmly talking me through until I got to grips with the clutch control and safely maneuvered it down the hill.

When the new school year began in August I was sad not to have Adéline around.

With Brad increasingly off being cool I would often hang out with Marie, crooning Gwen Stefani ballads in our bedrooms. After many evenings perfecting our harmonies we decided the time had come to take our act to the school stage. We had signed up for the strangely titled 'lip-singing' talent show and had our vocal performance all planned.

It was only on the day of the contest that we realized we'd made a huge mistake.

'It's lip-syncing not lip-singing!' I hissed at Marie, as we stood backstage watching a convoy of cool kids miming with perfect comic timing to songs like *Sweet Home Alabama*.

'I don't think we should go on stage,' I said to Marie. Unfortunately for me, she didn't listen.

Now that our well-prepared rendition of No Doubt's 'Don't Speak' with Marie singing lead and me harmonizing was of no use, all we could do was improvise. But while Marie did a great job of mouthing the words like a crestfallen Gwen I was left standing stiff on the stage in a Bon Jovi Shirt my Mom used to sleep in that I had altered to be off the shoulder and scattered with safety pins.

As 500 kids stared bemused at me it was clear I had to do something. So I started to sway, rock and twirl to the music. There I was, a regular Napoleon Dynamite, dancing like no one was watching in front of my whole school. Only everyone was watching, including a mortified Brad. For the next few weeks I continued to hang on to our relationship for dear life, despite the fact he continued to treat me like a social leper around his friends.

On September 11 2001 I was sitting in the front row of a math class when a member of staff came in and started whispering to my teacher. He immediately turned on the television. I was confused to see footage of the twin towers in New York on every channel. There was smoke billowing out of the side of one of the towers and, as we watched, a plane hit the second tower. I stared blankly at the screen. I didn't understand what was going on. When the first tower collapsed we were sent home from school.

I remember riding the bus home and feeling numb, shocked and really sad. When I walked into the trailer Mom had the TV on. She looked like she had been crying. I sat down next to her and watched for hours, feeling sick to my stomach.

Like many people I was left questioning life and instinctively wanted to be near to the people I loved. But when I finally spoke to Brad at school the next day he was acting really weird. He would not look me in the eye and seemed keen to get away from me.

'What's the matter?' I asked.

'I'm just upset about the trade center,' he shrugged.

A few days later my brother and I were in the kitchen.

'I saw Brad at the mall,' Tad said. 'He was at Taco Time kissing another girl.'

His words made me want to vomit.

'Don't lie,' I snapped. 'What girl?'

'Some skinny, blonde girl,' Tad replied. 'She isn't at our school.'

I'm not confrontational by nature so it took me a couple of sleepless nights before I finally had it out with Brad at school.

'Is it true?' I asked. 'Were you kissing someone else?'

'Yeah,' he said, finally meeting my eye. 'I don't want to be with you. I want to break up.' His coldness floored me. He was so just matter of fact about it.

I was crushed about our break-up and every time I saw Brad at school or at youth group it felt like my heart was being ripped from my chest all over again. I desperately wanted to understand his motives for ending it and cheating on me but I may as well have been invisible. As much as I pleaded Brad refused to talk to me.

I think part of the reason that it hurt me so deeply was his choice of rebound. She was blonde, and skinny, and popular. Everything I wasn't. My self-esteem was at an all-time low. Sometimes when I couldn't sleep I would get in my car late at night and drive past the house Brad now shared with his uncle. As I gazed up to see if his bedroom light was on I'd mournfully recall the time we'd banged in the bathroom while his grandmother banged around making sweet tea downstairs. Basically, every young woman's romantic dream. Sometimes I'd honk my horn out of spite, watching with vindictive glee as the lights flickered on. Sometimes I'd throw things in his yard. Trash usually. I never got caught.

Years later Brad messaged me out of the blue and apologized for the way he had treated me. I learned he was currently in the marines. The apology seemed out of character but it was such a nice gesture that I of course forgave him and didn't think of how strange the situation was. A week later I learned that Brad had taken his own life, hanging himself in his closet in the barracks. I still feel pangs knowing how alone he must have felt. I hope knowing that I harbored no animosity towards him brought him some peace. He still has a fond place in my heart.

Tess Holliday's Advice For Life #129:
Don't hang on to old feelings of hurt, the
only person you're hurting is yourself.

Tess Holliday's Advice for Life #136:
If you are ever feeling alone, please remember
you aren't. Suicide is a permanent solution
to a temporary feeling.

Probably the worst thing you can do when you've been dumped is go and get a radical haircut. So of course I went out and got a radical haircut. In a fit of spontaneity I cut my shoulder length hair into a short, spikey crop. I thought it would make me look edgy and angsty, but actually I looked like Bart Simpson.

I dyed it a purplish black with some grocery store box color, but there was no denying the it was just a bad haircut. This questionable move really didn't do me any favors visually or on the social ladder. Before long my old nickname 'Rhino' had been replaced by 'Porcupine' thanks to the incredibly creative kids on my bus.

'You look like a lesbian,' Susie announced when she spied my new do. 'A fat lesbian.'

Charming.

* * *

As 2001 limped to an end I got a job at a fast food joint called Ward's, famed for their chili dogs. I was paid $5.50 an hour to work on the front counter of the drive-thru, taking orders as the cars pulled up. Wards' slogan was 'Home of the Big One', which sounds very sexual. Every time I took an order I had to yell into a microphone, 'I need a big one' or 'I need a little one', which was kind of mortifying. Unsurprisingly truckers would often grin at me suggestively as they asked me just 'how big' I preferred it. Either way I didn't want it. Move it along, slugs.

It was not a glamorous job and every day I would go home with my black jeans and t-shirt stinking to high heaven of chili.

Half the fun of working at Ward's was my friend Eddie. Eddie was a chubby, mouthy guy with brown curly hair, who was kind of a more attractive version of Jack Black. He worked in the kitchen at Ward's and behaved atrociously. Eddie's favorite pastime was to play tricks on the other members of staff.

One day, as I raced to the kitchen to grab a foot-long chili dog for a customer, Eddie was waiting for me and slapped me full in the face with a hotdog wiener. I made the mistake of trying to chase him but my shoes were slippery from hotdog grease. Predictably I landed on my ass on the floor, smashing a mug in the process, while Eddie roared with laughter. As pranks went I got off lightly compared to the evil stunt Eddie pulled on a ditzy waitress he disliked. One of the 'perks' of the job was discounted food and when the girls in question put in an order for a burger I could see Eddie was plotting something despicable. I was horrified to see him throwing her burger on the ground and stepping on it. Then he sat in the back and laughed as she ate it. He did stuff like that to her ALL the time.

* * *

Just when my life felt like it could not get any crappier, a twister destroyed West Jones School.

Like much of the South, Laurel is situated at the mouth of 'Tornado Alley', a huge area of the USA stretching from Texas to Minneapolis where twisters are most frequent and deadly. Twice a year, as the weather begins to cool down or heat up rapidly, Mississippi is on high alert, awaiting the wrath of Mother Nature.

Whenever there is a risk of a tornado in your area the weather sirens sound with long, low notes reminiscent of air raid warnings. Normal TV shows are interrupted and the screen flashes black as a robotic voice announces 'Warning! Warning!' The local counties that are at risk are listed with details of the tornado's speed and direction. Anyone in the danger zone is urged to take cover. This may sound terrifying but when it happens multiple times a year throughout your childhood it doesn't feel like a big deal ... until, of course, it totals your high school. I don't know about you, but I think most kids have probably wished for something catastrophic to destroy their school – I definitely did! But when it happens it's actually kind of shocking.

If our school had been occupied at the time it could have been a catastrophic tragedy, but 'for the grace of God' (as Mom would say) we were all on spring break when the tornado hit. While no one was hurt, the storm attacked our school with fury, blowing holes through the classrooms and the gym and making it unusable for lessons. Two weeks later our classes were relocated to an old Walmart store down the street. Makeshift classroom walls were quickly erected out of plywood and my lessons began underneath obnoxious blue signs that read 'Everyday Low Price', which is about as classy as education gets. In fact, a lot of the old store signs were still hanging and I'm pretty sure it was a deliberate joke that the middle schoolers had their lessons in the 'diaper/baby' section.

Our Singers choir rehearsals took place in the loading docks (which admittedly had great acoustics – though I'm certain that was a coincidence) and the cafeteria was in the lawn and garden section of the store.

There were no ceilings above any of the classrooms so the atmosphere was noisy and chaotic. During classes Marie and I would relieve our boredom by throwing hand written letters over the top of the walls to each other.

It didn't take long for our school to be dubbed 'Walmart High' – a nickname embraced by the pupils of our rival school, Laurel High School, where Brad's new, shiny-haired girlfriend went. When our team played them at football they called the game 'the hicks versus the slicks' and it was all too embarrassing for words.

I spent most of my sophomore year heartbroken over Brad. Laurel was a small town and to my dismay I would see Brad and his new girlfriend often. Whenever I saw them outside the movies, at the mall or at a coffee shop, my heart would start to beat fast in my chest and a sick feeling would wash over me.

Desperate to get past the heartache I allowed my friend Ronnie, a girl I had met through mutual friends, to set me up. We were in the Piggly Wiggly parking lot listening to Incubus in her car when Ronnie's boyfriend arrived in his friend's truck.

'Go and hang out with Puddin',' Ronnie instructed as she made eyes at her beau. Reluctantly I headed over to Puddin's truck, which was lifted as high off its wheels as possible. Like many guys in the South, Puddin' was clearly using his truck as compensation for a perceived lack of masculinity. He gestured at me to climb in but didn't attempt to help me up (chivalry is dead in Laurel). After watching with amusement as I hauled my short ass into his cabin, Puddin' put on some awful country music and told me he worked in the oil fields. I guessed he was a couple of years older than me. He wasn't particularly attractive or interesting. After some small talk he leaned in for a kiss.

'Whatever,' I thought, going with the flow, but after a few seconds I was aware of something in my mouth. Ugh! It tasted rancid – like Tabasco and moldy leather.

Before I could stop myself I was gagging and I promptly threw up on his lap. For a fat girl five feet off the ground I exited his truck with surprising speed.

It was only afterwards that I realized that Puddin' had lunged for me with a mouth full of chewing tobacco. It was so gross. I never saw him again, obviously.

My summer job that year was at Subway where I had the grandiose title of 'sandwich artist'. I kid you not, I was not allowed to call myself anything else. Each shift it was my job to prep all the vegetables for the sandwiches. It was dull as hell and I hated being on my feet for my entire shift. In a stroke of lazy genius I countered this problem by sitting on an upside down bucket to give my legs a break. To pass the time I'd gorge on chocolate chip cookies or sneak bread, squirting on impressive amounts of mayo before eating it.

Most nights after 8pm Laurel was a ghost town, so Subway was where the shady characters and bored juvenile delinquents would come to hang out. Basically all the bad kids my mom told me not to hang out with would congregate at our store.

I had no pride in my job and my customer service was appalling. Being clumsy I cut my finger too many times to count and I would often have epic fights with my manager who wanted me to change my glove before I bled on the bread. The nerve! Any normal person would do this but I would stubbornly refuse. My attitude was terrible and I had no respect for my manager. I still had my heart set on working in fashion or as a make-up artist. I thought sandwich making was below me. What a little shithead.

Tess Holliday's Advice for Life #140:
Give every job 100% – nothing is beneath you.

One evening when, as usual, I had been giving my manager attitude, I got what I deserved. Halfway through my shift I saw a familiar figure on the sidewalk outside.

When Brad walked in with his uncle I nearly had an aneurysm. I ran to the back of the store in a panic. Brad could not see me like *this*. Not in a frumpy Subway shirt tucked into ill fitting black jeans. Not with bad hair and no make-up!

'Please don't make me serve him,' I begged my manager. 'He's my ex-boyfriend.'

'You're serving him,' he replied with a vindictive smirk.

Predictably Brad acted like he didn't know me. Trying not to cry, I hastily threw together Brad's sub and thrust it into his ungrateful hands.

* * *

When I returned to school in August we were back in our old school building. By now I was 17 and in the eleventh grade. I was planning to do one more year of school to get my high school diploma then I would be moving somewhere, *anywhere* that wasn't Laurel.

That first day I was excited to get back to Singers but when I walked into practice my jaw hit the floor. There was Brad sitting smiling amid MY friends. I had mentally steeled myself for seeing Brad again – but not at Singers.

'What are you doing here?' I asked, suddenly feeling short of breath.

'I joined,' he replied nonchalantly.

Dismay washed over me. The next hour was hell as my voice wobbled and my stomach churned at Brad's presence. I felt tearful and angry. Singers was the only thing I had that was mine. Why would be do this to me? There was no way I go to Singers every day and have him be there. It was too fucked. I walked out knowing I would never go back again.

Just when I thought my day could not get any worse I almost collided with Susie in the corridor. 'Gross,' she muttered looking me up and down.

That evening I told Mom I wanted to drop out.

'I want to be homeschooled,' I said. 'I can't do this any more.'

'Ryann, you're too old to be homeschooled,' she replied, not unkindly. 'Let me talk to your stepdad.'

Before the night was through a decision was made. I would leave West Jones and get my GED at an adult education school.

While Mom and Bill supported me, Dad was furious to discover I was dropping out. Tad had recently moved to Alabama with Dad insisting he complete eleventh grade at a local school. While my father had his faults, he was adamant that all his kids should finish their education.

'Do you want to be a loser?' he asked. 'You're going to be flipping burgers all your life.'

But after two years hating my summer jobs in the food industry I was confident I would not be opting for that career path. Even at 17 I had the foresight to know that to get a good job I needed qualifications. I resolved to work and study hard so that soon I would be done with my education for good.

My adult education school was ten minutes from my home in a nondescript building by a strip mall. There were people from all walks of life, ages and backgrounds and it definitely had its problems. A lot of the kids my age had been expelled from other schools. It was not unusual to overhear a stoned teenager attempting to deal weed during class. Then there were the volatile kids who would curse and shout and get into heated exchanges with the teachers. It wasn't an easy environment and I didn't always feel safe. Apart from making one friend, a girl called Amanda, I kept my head down. This school was a means to an end. After working hard for seven months I got my GED and left.

I never regretted dropping out of traditional education as I really had reached breaking point at West Jones High. My school experience sucked and I was never going to excel there. It wasn't working so I found an alternative.

I think for a lot of people school sucked and that's actually OK. School is just one part of your life and it doesn't have to set the scene for how the rest of your life will be. There should be no shame in changing a situation you're deeply unhappy with.

Tess Holliday's Advice for Life #147:
It's OK to drop out of school – it isn't for everyone.
There are many ways to get ahead in life, and you
can always come back to schooling if you want to.

Of course, sometimes I do wish I had stood up for myself more. If only I'd realized that eventually the kids who picked on me would have no power over me and I would leave them behind. If only I had known that one day my bullies would still live in the same miserable town and I'd be doing what I love for a living, traveling the world, modeling and promoting my own clothing line. But at the time I put my happiness in their hands.

I think I always knew I was destined to do things past my town (I was definitely desperate to leave), but I wish back then I could have embraced how unique I am.

I still have moments where I am propelled back to that feeling of worthlessness that I had at school. It's usually when I feel like I'm under scrutiny and not good enough.

Ironically two of the people who treated me like shit at school have since messaged me via Facebook to congratulate me on my achievements.

One even wrote: 'You always were awesome and I knew you'd do it.'

I probably would have let bygones be bygones if she had bothered to apologize but the lack of acknowledgement of the suffering she caused me made me angry.

'You should really think about the ramifications of your behavior,' I replied. 'You really hurt me at school and you need to think about that.'

I never got the apology but that's OK.

Nick is really good at reminding me to believe in myself and not to care what people think. It is hard, though. It's so ingrained in me to care, but I know he is right, those people don't matter, you don't have to impress everyone.

When you set yourself free like that it's easy to be resilient.

Chapter 6

Small Town, Small Minds

So I was itching to get out of Laurel. The way Brad had treated me had damaged my self-esteem and my hometown was full of unwanted reminders of our relationship. Sometimes, when I had a flashback to his criticisms of my body, I could be pretty self-loathing.

'You look disgusting,' I'd tell myself in my lowest moments. 'You're so gross.'

I hated that being stuck in Laurel brought out these kind of negative feelings. Why did I feel a need to be so hard on myself? If I didn't *want* to feel this way, it was down to me to make a change. I am a big believer that if something isn't working in your life you have to make a proactive decision to be bold and step outside your comfort zone. Bit by bit, the realization had dawned on me that I needed to spread my wings and get out of Laurel. That was the only way I could start to learn to love myself and feel empowered.

As well as the bad feelings about Brad I was feeling low after inadvertently unleashing a storm at our church.

Things had come to head when I had invited Amanda, my friend from my GED classes, to come to church with her boyfriend Timmylou.

That Sunday the three of us arrived for the service and sat towards the back. Amanda and Timmylou behaved impeccably, singing along to the hymns even if they didn't know them and listening intently to the sermon. But after the service I was aware of a feeling of tension in the church. Not one person came up and spoke to us and I could feel disapproving eyes burning into us. A feeling of dismay came over me; were they reacting like this because Timmylou was black?

A couple of days later Mom, Tad and I were sat at the kitchen table eating dinner when the phone rang. Mom answered and I saw her face fall.

'I thought the Bible said, "Go ye therefore and preach unto all nations", not just to white people?' she replied before hanging up. She was visibly upset.

'Who was that?' I asked.

'I don't know,' she said. 'They asked me what my daughter was trying to prove by bringing *those kind* of people into our church.'

When I heard the words I felt shocked, saddened and angry. I desperately wanted to be wrong about the reaction to Timmylou but now my fear had been confirmed. Were some of the people we celebrated our faith with every Sunday really that prejudiced? It seemed the answer was yes and I was done.

It hit Mom hard too and she also vowed never to return. Her faith was strong but the injustice of the situation rattled her. Regrettably the drama caused some tension with my grandparents who pleaded with Mom to let it go. They had been going to the church all their lives and their parents were buried in the church's cemetery. They were embarrassed by the fall out but Mom would not budge. She probably could have returned without being ostracized but she never set foot in that church again. Eventually she found a new church and congregation who welcomed her into the fold. I am still proud of her for standing her ground over a despicable attitude of racism towards people her daughter valued dearly.

Sick to the back teeth of small-minded Laurel, I quit my job at Subway and moved to Woodstock, Alabama, to live with my dad, his wife Lisa and my growing brood of brothers. Gabriel was now three and Lisa had recently given birth to my littlest brother Hunter. Seeing as Tad, who was not crazy about toddlers or babies, had his own converted room above the garage, Dad had promised to let me have the guest bedroom.

The town of Woodstock was even smaller than Laurel with one stop light, one grocery store, a Subway, a post office and little else to write home about. I probably would have gone stir crazy but thankfully Woodstock was a mere 30 miles from Birmingham, Alabama, a big city with a population of 233,000. It had good restaurants, movie theatres and big malls. Best of all, no one knew me there.

It didn't take me long to get a full-time job as a teller in a bank. The work could be pretty mundane but it was so much better than being a 'sandwich artist'. Working at the bank provided me with a modest income and I enjoyed the freedom of coming and going without being questioned by Dad or Lisa.

Admittedly it was far from a calm household. My half-brothers Gabriel and Hunter were high maintenance and on top of their toddler tantrums we had my dad's! To be fair, Lisa handled Dad pretty well considering how awful he could be. Instead of getting emotional like my mom she would give as good as she got. On more than one occasion I heard her declare, 'Fuck you. You're an asshole,' and walk out the house. She was great at shutting Dad down when he was being unreasonable. Still, it was an emotional rollercoaster as Dad did his usual trick of flitting between moments of kindness (like painting my bedroom black and hot pink as a surprise) and then losing his temper and making me feel shit about myself.

Sadly when Dad was being nice I usually suspected there was an ulterior motive. I should have smelt a rat when he quickly agreed to be the legal owner of my car in return for one 'small condition'. Now that I was earning I had my heart set on a brand-new Honda Civic. I didn't have the credit rating to get approved by myself so I needed Dad to be named on the payment agreement.

'I'll do it,' he said. 'If you tell your Mom I don't have to legally support you any more.'

It didn't seem like a big deal seeing as I'd already left home so naively I agreed. Dad signed up to the car payments with the arrangement that I would pay each monthly installment.

'I'll even pay you extra money each month,' I promised. 'That way if I anything goes wrong I'll have the money saved.'

After we'd got the car Dad handed me a document to sign, and I hastily scribbled my signature. Turns out I made a bad bargain and he stopped paying for my health-care. He was supposed to be paying it until I was 24. You stay classy! I may have been sold down the river but I loved my new car. It was the first nice thing I had ever owned so I felt really fancy as I drove with the sunroof down, singing along to The Killers. From Dad's place in Woodstock it took me two-and-half hours to drive home to Laurel so I would often spend weekends back in Missis-sippi with Mom. She and Bill had recently finished doing up her first home, which she had lived in as a child before my grandparents moved into the family farmhouse.

While I was home I often sought out Eddie at Ward's to catch up on the latest Laurel news. There was usually someone I knew who had been busted by the cops for drugs or who had got in a car wreck. One weekend Eddie pulled up his work t-shirt to show me his chest.

'Look what I got done,' he said, pointing proudly. Each of his scrawny man nipples had a safety pin through them. 'Want me to pierce yours?'

I shrugged, feeling indifferent. I already had several piercings in my ears. How painful could it be? When Eddie's shift was over we headed to a Mississippi State Park bathroom.

'Just do one to start with,' I instructed as a laughing Eddie inspected a cleanish safety pin. I hitched up my top.

'Oh gross your boob!' Eddie exclaimed, before pushing the pin through my nipple with sadistic force.

Fuck! It burnt so bad. Afterwards I sat in Eddie's car cradling my injured boob while he laughed at me. He bought be a peach soda to console me, but it didn't make my chest throb any less.

It was past midnight when I arrived home and fell into bed. I tried to sleep but my maimed boob was throbbing like a bitch. I held out for six hours before I had to get a pair of tweezers and pushout the safety pin. Amazingly, I did not get an infection. That was the first and last time I attempted to pierce my nipples. Instead, clearly learning little from my mistake, I went for something more permanent.

In Mississippi, getting your first tattoo is almost a mandatory teenage rite of passage. Cheap tattoo parlors are everywhere in the South, dispensing an array of body art that is usually crappy or patriotic or both. We're talking tattoos of guns with the words 'Southern Pride' or a Tasmanian devil wrapped in the Confederate flag. My dad likes to think outside the box and wanted a Tasmanian devil riding a motorbike. That is until I reminded him he didn't own a motorcycle.

So I got my first tattoo on my eighteenth birthday in Hattiesburg, Mississippi – and my mom took me to get it. Like many God-fearing Southern gals, Mom had a bunch of tattoos that followed a Christian theme, but were not done well. The 'salvation bracelet' on her wrist didn't even stretch all the way round and the cross on her ankle looked more like the logo of Pabst Blue Ribbon beer. While some people thought this was pretty cool (liquor tattoos are also a Southern staple) it wasn't exactly the result she was looking for. I knew she was hoping my first tattoo would depict something Godly and celestial.

Humoring her enthusiasm for visual tributes to Jesus I ran my eyes over the Bible-inspired section of tattoo art. Then while she was distracted I picked out a risqué fairy. She had a dirty look and one boob hanging out.

'I want it in pastel colors,' I told the tattoo artist, who I had the feeling was fresh out of prison. I later confirmed my suspicions about his time in the slammer, but what the hell – that's where most tattooists in the South hone their skills.

'That's a great idea!' he replied, clearly not giving a flying fart that pastel colored tattoos are notorious for fading.

I sat in his tiny, hot studio trying not to flinch as he got to work on my shoulder. I was surprised it didn't really hurt. It didn't feel good, but it was nowhere near the hell of Eddie piercing my nipple. Tattoo pain is kind of like having sunburn and someone stabbing the tender area with a butter knife. Imagine a prickly, uncomfortable JAB JAB JAB. I tried to distract myself by silently judging the girl opposite me. She was getting a small playboy bunny with a camouflage bow on her back.

What a fucking loser,' I thought, unaware of the irony as I waited for my multicolored, slut fairy to flutter to life. Tattoos can be deeply meaningful or completely ridiculous, and no one approach is any better than another. I have a mixture of both. Do I regret any? Sure, kind of, but mainly because I was impatient and didn't wait for the right artist to make my ideas bloom on my skin.

Tess Holliday's Advice for Life #151: Cheap tattoos aren't good and good tattoos aren't cheap.

When I returned to Alabama I was so proud of my little winged companion. I pulled pouty poses over my shoulder as I studied her in the mirror. This was my first experience of how getting tattooed could give me a welcome boost of self-esteem. Even now, with half my body covered in artwork, I still love having a new tattoo. Each one feels like I am adding a chapter to a living journal on my body. They remind me of the places I got them and the people I got them with. They remind me to feel brave, beautiful and bold – plus they make for good stories over a glass of whiskey.

* * *

Most days, once I had finished my shift at the bank in Birmingham, I would head home and retreat to my bedroom to watch *Sex and the City* on HBO. What a party animal! One night, however, I reluctantly headed out to a club with my colleague Annie. After a night of dancing, shaking every last curve I had to Britney Spears, I followed the party back to Annie's boyfriend's place. He lived with his parents so the plan was to continue the party in the fully furnished basement. When we arrived at the house the power had gone out. I followed Annie down the stairs via a cell phone light, wondering if I should leave. In true 2004 fashion, I was buzzed from a few too many vodka red bulls, and stumbling a little I felt my way to sit on a large leather couch. Perhaps my drunkenness is why the evening transpired the way it did. My inexperience and insecurity certainly didn't help either.

'Hi,' I heard a male voice say next to me. I couldn't see him as it was pitch black but knew that Annie's boyfriend had been hanging out with friends from a nearby Army base.

'I have a blanket,' the voice added. 'I'll share it with you.'

'I'm fine,' I replied.

'I won't touch you,' he insisted. 'We'll just share a blanket.'

I relented and he moved in close. Within a couple of minutes he was trying to kiss me. It was pretty fucked up as I had no idea what he looked like but perversely the weirdness of the situation kind of turned me on. I kissed him back. One thing led to another and soon we were having sex on the couch. We didn't use protection and there were other people in the room. We were trying to be quiet but because the couch was leather I kept sticking to it, making obvious, squeaky noises.

Eventually I fell asleep and when I woke up the lights were back on. I realized the guy I'd had sex with was sitting near me, as he kept giving me shifty sideways glances. He wasn't completely unattractive but with him now pretending I didn't exist I felt objectified and embarrassed so I left. I didn't even stop to find out his name.

As I showered back at Dad's I wondered what I'd been thinking. What sort of danger had I put myself in? Why hadn't I removed myself from the situation when I felt unsafe?

The next time I was home in Laurel I sheepishly told Eddie about the events of that night.

'You're really lucky you didn't get pregnant,' he said. 'Imagine if you did and your kid asked, "What does my dad look like?" You'd have to turn off the light and feel your kid's face to give an answer.'

Tess Holliday's Advice for Life #155:
If it sounds like something you'd read
in a book with Fabio on the cover, it's
probably a bad idea in real life.

Determined to try to find my confidence I started to experiment more with my style. I had recently got into the music and social networking website MySpace where I was introduced to alternative, tattooed models. They were sexy, pushing boundaries with what was deemed acceptable by society, and they oozed femininity. A couple of things I now knew for sure, were that I wanted to be just like them, and I wanted way more tattoos.

Finally I decided on something I considered pretty fucking profound for my next tattoo – the word 'unique' on my left arm. Hadn't Mom always told me I was named Ryann because I was 'unique' and 'different'? There was no denying that having a gender-neutral name made me stand out. In the South every other kid had a name like Sarah-Anne or Misty so being called Ryann always raised eyebrows. When you think about it, my mom was actually being quite progressive. And despite the teasing, I went on to give both my children gender-neutral monikers.

Tess Holliday's Advice for Life #159:
Be the parent that you needed when you
were a child. Also, if you have a stupid
name just make it a family tradition.

Before I had my tattoo done I thought about the lettering I wanted. Then I walked into a makeshift tattoo shop in a trailer in Woodstock and instructed the guy to put 'type-writer lettering' on my arm. I didn't even consider whether he was reputable or possibly about to give me hepatitis.

'I don't do typewriter fonts,' he drawled, pointing me towards his years out of date computer. 'Y'all gonna have to pick out a font you want on there.'

Any normal person would run out the door at this point but stubborn little old me was like, 'That seems like a GREAT idea!' I quickly found an ill-conceived alien font on Microsoft Word and let him loose on my skin. After 20 minutes he stood back to admire his efforts and I got to see his awful handiwork.

I returned to the epicenter of our teenage universe – the Winn-Dixie parking lot – and triumphantly unveiled my new pride and joy to Eddie.

'What the fuck is that?' he spat, falling into fits of laughter. 'And who is Linique!?'

The letters were so crooked and close together that it seemed to spell the name Linique. As we chatted Eddie told me about two new chicks he'd met named Sarah and Heather.

'They're from Seattle and they work at Waffle House,' he explained. 'They're fucking weirdos like you.'

As a social pariah I wasn't stoked on meeting new people, but begrudgingly agreed to hang out with Eddie's new friends. Damn it, Eddie had good taste. Sarah and Heather, who were best friends born and raised in Seattle, were definitely a breath of fresh air for Laurel.

Sarah was a cool, casual girl who mostly wore jeans and a band-emblazoned shirt. Meanwhile Heather's style was vintage chic. She was always customizing clothes she'd found at Goodwill or thrift stores and loved Victorian style shoes and Cameo jewelry.

While Eddie cracked jokes to Sarah (they went on to date and eventually married) I chatted to Heather. We quickly bonded over our mutual love of Tank Girl comic books and Rat Fink art.

'Why the fuck did you decided to come to Laurel?' I asked.

'We're here for the "Southern experience", she laughed. 'Plus Sarah's grandfather lives here and said we could stay.'

'I love how different the South is,' she added. 'Compared to Seattle it's like another country here.'

When Heather talked about the West coast and the other places she had visited like New York City, I admired her adventurous attitude. The envy I felt also confirmed a nagging feeling – I was growing bored of Alabama. For many years I had been harboring a feeling of wanderlust and now I was dying to escape the South altogether.

I'd always known other parts of America were different – the good God-fearing folks of Laurel certainly liked to take the moral high ground about that! It was often said that everyone outside the South was a sinner and going to hell. But even in my sheltered Southern bubble I knew that Mississippi was backward. Where we lived we only had dial-up internet available and no one admitted to watching racy HBO dramas for fear of being judged. There was so much sexual suppression. I suspected a lot of people were secretly hiding dog-eared romance novels and 'personal massagers' under their mattress.

'You should definitely come to visit me in Seattle,' Heather said. 'You'd love what a contrast it is.' Her encouragement emboldened me. I made up my mind then and there that I would make it happen.

With Eddie's ridicule of my latest tattoo still eating at me, I made an impromptu visit to the Mississippi artist who had tattooed my poorly rendered fairy.

'Can you add some shading?' I asked. 'I want the letters to stand out more.'

On my instruction he put hot pink around the letters then black around the hot pink. I told myself I was happy with it because I *loved* hot pink. In reality it was still an abomination that still looked like the imaginary name Linique, but now with what looked vaguely like colorful bruises around it. That was far from the last time I tried to correct that god-forsaken tattoo. I took it to another questionable shop to see what (if anything) could be done to fix it.

'I could put a coffin over it here,' suggested a weathered-faced man, his fingers circling an outline of almost my entire ample forearm. No good tattoo artist would ever suggest shading in half of someone's arm, but I went with it. And that is how I came to have a somewhat geometric black blob with added bat wings on my arm. There was one silver lining: no one calls me Linique any more.

Since then there have been two more ill fated attempts to improve my tattoo. The coffin has been lightened with white and grey and what turned out to be a somewhat anatomically *incorrect* heart has been added. To date I've had four tattooers work on it, at a cost of at least a thousand dollars, and it's still pretty goddamn awful.

Tess Holliday's Advice for Life #166:
You can't polish a turd, and if you try you'll
probably end up with some shit on you.

'Where is this garbage tattoo?' you may ask. 'Why haven't I spotted it on Instagram?'

Nice try asshat. You will NEVER see the inside of my left arm. I intend to keep it out of shot until the day I finally have it removed by laser. My big plan is to replace it with traditional tattoo flash art from the 1950s. We'll see how that works out. I made my coffin, so to speak, and for now I have to lie in it. At least it amuses Nick.

I kept in touch with Heather, who was shortly heading back up west to Washington. Determined to take her up on her offer I had wasted no time in booking a flight to Seattle.

Getting away for a few days was going to be a welcome break. Living with Dad, who was constantly tired from running around after two children under four, was becoming a strain. He was always shouting at someone and I hated the hostile atmosphere.

The weekend of my big trip finally arrived and I held my breath as the plane ascended upwards through the clouds. It was my first experience of flying and I was both scared and close to peeing myself with excitement.

Looked down at the ground from 40,000 feet was my first real perspective of how big the world is. Brilliant sunshine poured through the small oval window of the plane, filling me with optimism. It felt like the world was my oyster. I'd always wanted to escape the South and for the first time I felt free and independent.

Five hours later I arrived in Seattle where Heather met me off the plane. As we drove to her parents' home I fell in love with the city immediately. It was just as beautiful as Heather had described.

'It's so green,' I marveled, my eyes glued to the window. The size of the evergreen and fir trees blew my mind.

At Heather's home we were immediately warmly welcomed by her parents, Steve and Rose. They did not have a big home but had kindly made room for me to sleep on the couch. As well as Heather they had two sons; Nate, who was older than Heather and had his own place, and her little brother Willie, who could usually be found eating jello pudding out of a bowl and playing video games.

For the next four days Heather gave me her person-alized tour of the city and I marveled at how different everybody seemed. Seattleites had a lot of personality and were comically unapologetic. I couldn't get over how cosmopolitan the city was. Prior to my visit to Seattle I had never tried Greek food but suddenly I was eating a fancy chickpea dip called hummus! What is this fancy foreign delight? I would come to learn in time that this exotic concoction is in reality available at most super-markets – at least once you pass the Mason Dixon line. I also had Asian food for the first time, trying not to choke at the spiciness of a Thai red curry.

'I want to move here,' I told Heather on my last day. 'I'm definitely done with Alabama.'

'If you like it here, you should do it!' she agreed. 'I think you would be happy.'

We headed back to the house, giddy with the excite-ment of my plan to make Seattle home.

Arriving back in Birmingham after the best vacation of my life, I was relieved to have the house to myself. Dad, Lisa and my two young brothers had headed off on a trip of their own leaving me with peace and quiet and time to think. After such a happy weekend in Seattle watching Heather interact with her father I was dreading being back in the company of mine. Her family life seemed so perfect. I had not heard Steve criticize Heather once and he seemed so proud and supportive of all his kids.

On a whim, I packed up my belongings and persuaded a friend to let me stay in her trailer for a few days. I would give my two weeks notice at the bank and then relocate to Seattle. I spent my last few weeks in Alabama couch surfing with friends before returning to Laurel to prepare for my move. As I suspected my dad reacted with cold indifference to my sudden departure and seemed unfazed by the news of my big move.

Mom meanwhile failed miserably in her attempts to put on a brave face.

'I always knew you'd want to live somewhere else,' she said with tears in her eyes. 'I'll miss you, but I'm proud of you.'

In September 2004, Heather flew into New Orleans airport ready to accompany me on my epic road trip to Seattle. We would be setting off from Laurel, driving a scenic route of approximately 3,000 miles through Louisiana, Texas, New Mexico, Arizona, California, Oregon and Washington.

'You drive carefully… I love you child' Mom earnestly told me after I'd shoved the last of my meager belongings into the car. 'Make sure you call me ALL the time.'

We both cried as she engulfed me in a bear hug.

Our first stop on the journey was Shreveport, Louisiana, where we planned to stay with Heather's friend whose husband was stationed there in the military. After dinner with the couple we headed back to the military base where a bunch of macho looking marines were relaxing outside in folding chairs. They eyed us curiously and suddenly our host seemed uneasy.

'I'm sorry but I don't think it's a good idea for you to stay here,' he said, looking me up and down.

'Some of the guys can be pretty opinionated and they will probably be mean to you… uh… because of your size.'

Wow. I hadn't seen that coming. Flushing red, I turned to Heather. Somewhat reluctantly she agreed to leave and we headed to the car. As we drove in silence to a dodgy motel I felt so hurt. Being turned away for my size had cut me deeply but Heather's reaction stung even more. I felt like she was mad with me, like somehow it was my fault. I was angry that my weight was an issue but I couldn't bear to have it out with her. It was all too humiliating. The next morning Heather was back to her smiley, optimistic self, so I didn't bring it up. It was not our first or last drama of the trip.

Tess Holliday's Advice for Life #168:
Fight for who you are and what you believe in.
Even if it seems small, it's worth it.

The following day we crossed the border into Texas, taking it in turns to drive or nap.

Eight hours in, it was my turn to take the wheel but as we neared the city of Amarillo I found the road signs taxing. The speed limit would regularly change from 60 mph to 30 mph then back to 60 mph and so on. I thought I had been paying close attention but around midnight I was shocked to see flashing blue lights behind me. I pulled to the curb gritting my teeth and silently praying I would not get a ticket.

'Do you know why I pulled you over?' a cop in his late twenties asked when he got to my window.

'No,' I replied, while Heather also shook her head with wide-eyed innocence.

I was sure he was going to book me but after a little smooth talking from Heather he appeared to have had a change of heart.

'I'll let you go on your way,' he declared to my surprise.

We thanked him profusely but Heather being Heather she continued to make small talk. She certainly charmed him because before I knew it I was taking a photo of her and the grinning police officer for her travel journal.

On a high after our close shave with the law we decided to take a quick detour into Oklahoma so we could add another state to our list. By now it was 2am and, pulling into a tiny town, we found a horde of bored looking teenagers.

Heather quickly befriended them, true to form, and one suggested we play ding dong ditch. For those not familiar with the game, we snuck up to stranger's houses, rang their doorbells and then ran off into the night. After cruelly disturbing the sleep of a bunch of innocent Oklahomans we got back in the car and kept on driving. By the time we arrived in Bernaillo, New Mexico, we had travelled 850 miles in 24 hours.

In the following days we often discovered our trip was far from well thought out. Plans to camp in Arizona were immediately shelved when we spotted signs warning about poisonous snakes and scorpions. Traveling through California we narrowly missed forest fires and were shocked by the charred-looking mountains in Santa Barbara. Ironically, seeing as I now live here, I was bitterly disappointed by Los Angeles. My overriding impression was that it was dirty and expensive and nothing like it seemed in the movies. Come to think of it, that's all still true. But you learn to love it's quirks.

Finally, after 15 days on the road, we crossed the state border into Washington. As all around nature encompassed us with tall, green, luscious beauty we began to see the road signs for Seattle. As we drove the last hundred miles towards my new adventurous life on the West coast I felt happy and energized. At last I was facing life head on and being brave. It felt awesome.

Chapter 7

Ryann the Girl

When I summoned up the courage to move to Seattle I will admit that at first I saw it as the answer to all my problems. Seattle's city culture was cool and alternative, the weather was agreeable and the people were more like me. Naively I assumed I would instantly slip into life there and make my mark in a new city, thousands of miles from home.

Tess Holliday's Advice for Life #168:
A change of scenery is nice, but your problems
will follow you. Change has to be internal first.

I can see now that I was so obsessed with escaping the south and reinventing myself that it didn't really occur to me that my challenge was just beginning. I never stopped to think how my actions or decisions could shape my future. However, there's no denying that I had fallen on my feet thanks to Heather's family. Her parents, Steve and Rose, were so welcoming. They invited me into their home rent-free and treated me like one of their own. The

Cozad family lived in Covington, a quiet neighborhood 30 minutes from the city, with lush greenery all around. Once again I took up residence in the family's living room, sleeping on the couch and stashing my stuff in Heather's room.

After Mississippi's relentless sun and suffocating heat it was easy to love Seattle. Most of the time the temperature was about 50 F, overcast and misting. It rained 70 per cent of the time, but I loved walking around feeling fresh and rejuvenated. During high summer in Laurel I'd struggled to walk 200 feet when the claustrophobic heat hit. It felt like I could pass out any moment.

Heather, having inherited her parents' open and generous nature, quickly introduced me to her circle of friends. I was lucky to be welcomed into the pack. People in Seattle are known to be standoffish and transplants to the city often complain about the 'Seattle freeze', a phenomenon that sees locals reacting with an aloof disinterest to newbies. Hailing from the South, where everyone is into everyone else's business or ready to spill out their heart (any good country music song will tell you that) it was a surprise to discover that Seattleites by nature are far too cool to ask ten million questions about your life.

While one-upmanship in the South revolved around money, faith and family, in Seattle everyone seemed to be attempting to be more alternative than the next person. A true Seattlelite millennial liked to listen to obscure bands up until the point they became 'too mainstream' and expressed themselves creatively by gluing shit like Barbie doll heads to their car. They were both health conscious and culinary snobs, owned a compost garden, grew their own vegetables and had the trendiest dog on the block. But, while it could be pretty pretentious, I actually enjoyed the quirky, bohemian vibe of Seattle. The posh (grass-fed, organic meat) burgers were good and I liked the eccentric, outspoken people.

For the first time in my life I felt part of a cool gang. Heather and I spent our time with like-minded hipster-types going to gigs, burlesque and art shows and hanging out in independent coffee shops and book stores. Although all these things genuinely sparked my interest, at times I would sit there feeling like an imposter. Listening to my new friends talking often felt like a cultural orientation to the West coast. They were always referencing bands, obscure music and movies with the assumption everyone in the room knew them. Often I'd make a mental note to go home and Google them.

Most embarrassing of all was my internal reaction when the conversation drifted to topics such as evolution, Darwinism and the Stone Age. I would listen intently, my mind blown. Oh yes, it took me moving to Seattle at the age of 18 to finally discover that dinosaurs were real and cavemen existed. Of course I never let on how selective my childhood education had really been.

After leaving Mississippi feeling very jaded about my faith I was intrigued to see Heather embracing religion in an altogether different way to the version of Christianity I had experienced in the south. Like most of her friends, Heather was a Christian, but not in the 'convert everyone' way I was used to in Laurel. She was a cool, laid-back Christian who listened to post-hardcore Christian rock. Her favorite band was called Emery. When she played them to me they sounded like scream metal with no overtly religious overtones. I grew to love them too.

The Cozads' church was small and welcoming, but, while I accompanied the family to Sunday morning service a few times, I did not become an active member of the congregation. While I had a faith – and I probably still do – I wanted to keep a healthy distance from organized religion and the beliefs and rules set out by the church. I felt that it was time for me to discover my own viewpoints of the world. Religion and guilt had dominated that aspect of my life for too long.

Living with Heather's family was easy. The Cozad house was a hotbed of happy and creative energy. At the weekends, Heather was always customizing cool outfits, while Rose decorated china for a hobby and Steve painted miniature civil war soldiers, horses or warplanes. As I sat by the fire making rag dolls with Heather, it felt nice to be part of a family that felt like the ones I had seen on TV. My Mom always did her very best, but most of the men around me growing up always ensured I could never really feel safe.

In stark contrast it was not unusual for Steve to sit at the kitchen table and ask with genuine interest what I wanted to do with my life. At first I was cautious, wondering why he was asking me. I was scared to open up and pour out my heart because of the way my own dad used to belittle me. But after a while I realized that this was what kind and caring fathers did. Steve never made fun or poured scorn on my plans. He encouraged me to think big and go out and achieve my goals. To him, this probably didn't seem like a big deal, but it certainly had a big effect on me. Having grown up with a lack of positive male role models in my life, it meant the world that Steve cared about me and treated me like his own daughter. He asked me how my day was and gently made it clear when he didn't approve of things. In many ways he was more of a father to me than my own dad, which is probably why I dragged my feet about moving out for so long.

After moving to Seattle to be independent, it turned out I was extremely *dependent* on Rose and Steve. I'm sure I would start to lose patience with a friend of my child crashing on the couch for five nights let alone five months, but Rose and Steve went above and beyond. They are the kind of people who will do anything for anyone and to be honest I took advantage of their hospitality for far too long.

While my weekends were filled with fun adventures exploring Seattle with Heather, I had some serious hours to kill during the week when Heather was studying at

Seattle Pacific University and Steve was at work. Rose was often occupied as she was a full-time carer for her ageing father, Harlan, who had Parkinson's Disease.

When no one else was around I would spend most of the day in Steve's office using the family computer to 'job search'. In truth, after 30 minutes flitting half-heartedly around employment sites I would inevitably fall down the rabbit hole and log on to MySpace.

I'd click around trying to find contacts in the modeling industry and while away the hours chatting to alternative models and photographers. Most days I would borrow Steve's digital camera and shoot dozens of 'carefree' shots in the hope some would be good enough to upload.

While my online persona, 'Ryann The Girl', was bright and brash and embraced her curves, I was rarely happy with the pictures and no amount of snapping away would stop my critical internal dialogue. I still had hang ups about myself and my eyes would always focus on the parts of my body in the photo I disliked the most. Above all it was my arms that I struggled with. The way I saw it they were large and disproportional to the rest of me and I hated having them out for people to see. For the longest time I had relied on long-sleeved cardigans and sweaters to hide them – even in scorching 90 F Southern summers. Up until Seattle, my life had felt like an extra-long, hideous Bikram yoga class.

I was always posing and preening for photos but the confident moments caught on camera more often than not

My favorite photo of my parents, plus look at my mom's glow!

My mom helping me with my dress, I was about four here.

Jeremy, my brother Tad, myself and Mandy. My mom even got us all matching outfits... gotta love the 80's!

Tina Tidwell, my godmom. I miss her everyday.

My brother Tad and I at the zoo. You can see how uncomfortable I was in my body. Sadly.

AUGUST
1999

Me at age 16 –
the porcupine hair
makes a debut!

I like to title this one
"Preggo Prison". You
can see the prison was
literally in my backyard!

Me as a new
mom with Rylee
asleep on me in
my grandparents'
living room in
Mississippi.

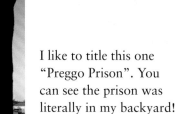

Where it all starts… my first photoshoot (nude too!), shot by Elizabeth Raab in Seattle. © Elizabeth Raab

Rylee, or as I call him "Nugget", and his teddy bear/ best friend Baby in 2013 in our first home by ourselves in Pasadena, CA.

The moment Nick proposed to me at Flinders Street Station in a Photo Booth in Melbourne, Australia, 2014.

Instagram/Tess Holliday

Mine and
Nick's Vegas
Wedding!
We have fun
together!

Little Church of the West
WEDDING
CHAPEL

Bowie and Rylee snuggled up at our home in Long Beach, CA, 2017.

Celebrating our first wedding anniversary at the Madonna Inn in San Luis Obipso, CA.

hid negative thoughts about myself. Instead of appreciating a special moment, like a snap of Mom and I hugging goodbye right before I left Laurel, I'd think, 'Ugh, I never should have posed at that angle. I look so fat.'

My body image was volatile to say the least. Deep down I knew that the body I was in WAS my norm. I really wanted to celebrate that, but I didn't quite know how. I still had a lot to learn about loving myself.

Each day, when Steve arrived home from his job as a carpenter, he would find me sat in the exact same place he'd left me – on the computer, on MySpace. It was obvious that sitting around in front of the computer all day had left me feeling wired and irritable.

'Is this really the best use of your time?' he asked me more than once after discovering 101 pouting selfies clogging up his camera memory. 'Why don't you go outside, take a walk and get some fresh air? I think you need to do something other than work on your vanity.'

He wasn't being mean, just candid. His advice definitely came from a good place. He knew that I had come to Seattle to start a new life but yet here I was hiding from the real world, wasting each day on the internet. Steve wanted me to live my life, to get out my comfort zone and be proactive. And, let's be honest, they probably wanted me out from under their feet too! Often he'd come home to give me some words of tough love and it was exactly what I needed. At times I am my own worst enemy when it comes to taking a leap in my life that will ultimately get me to where I want to be. I can be stubborn and hesitant but I definitely don't like it when my procrastination is pointed out to me. But nobody thrives if they just have people in their life who tell them what they want to hear. It's important to have people around who are prepared to challenge you, even if it initially rubs you the wrong way.

It's funny as I have married someone who is just like that. I get mad at Nick when he tells me to try harder or to step out my comfort zone but deep down I know he is right. Some of my best decisions have come from his encouragement and annoying Australian bluntness. Likewise, when I was hiding in cyberspace, Steve gave me a push in the right direction to go out and face the real world. Eventually I got off my ass and found a job.

My new position was at Lane Bryant, the store where Mom had bought me my first 'grown up' outfits. I'd loved the clothes and the ethos of the brand ever since, so I really didn't care that the hours were crappy and the pay was paltry. My store was located inside a mall in north Seattle and we had a steady flow of customers. I took to the job straight away as I loved meeting women shaped like me and helping them to find something they felt great in.

My new income meant I could finally give Rose and Steve their living room back and I rented a room in a tiny apartment in a shitty part of town behind a Taco Bell. Trust me, that wasn't a coincidence. I missed the Cozads but it felt good to be independent and supporting myself for the very first time.

I had been working at Lane Bryant for a couple of months when a customer with purple hair caught my attention. She was easily a US size 20 and had tattoos everywhere, including on her hands and her neck. As I assisted her in the changing rooms I admired the way she seemed so confident and comfortable with her body.

'I always hide my arms,' I admitted, as she posed in front of the mirror in a sleeveless tank top. 'I'll wear a cardigan so people don't see how big they are.'

I wasn't entirely sure why I was unburdening my hang-ups to a complete stranger but she went with it.

'That's why I started tattooing my arms,' she said. 'Now I love showing them off.'

As she sashayed confidently out of the store she left me thinking about her positive body attitude – I hoped one day I could be like that too.

Tess Holliday Advice for Life #170:
Embrace and celebrate your jiggly, wobbly
weirdly textured parts, and modify or adorn your
body however you damn please. It's yours
and nobody else's opinion matters.

Since arriving in Seattle my look had changed a lot. I had dyed my hair red and cut short, rockabilly-style 'betty bangs'. I had honed my style to be a nod to the curvy, pin-up era but with a contemporary twist thanks to the 'snakebite' lip piercings I'd added to both sides of my bottom lip. My favorite outfits consisted of eye-catching polka dot and leopard-skin items that Heather and I had discovered at vintage and thrift stores across Seattle.

My days of surfing MySpace paid off when Misha, a photographer I'd met online, offered to take some free photos of me in return for using them to promote her work. I jumped at the chance of some professional shots so one weekend we did a goth-style shoot. The photos, which consisted of shots of me peeking seductively through a curtain and lying on the ground, were much more edgy than I'd had done before with not a silver shirt or cowhide clog in sight (cringe).

I had proudly uploaded them to my MySpace page, listing myself as an 'alternative model'. It quickly resulted in a new flow of traffic to my page and complimentary (if often suggestive) messages filling my inbox. For the first time since Brad, I began to feel sexy, and getting male attention to validate that was addictive.

One night, I joined Heather and a bunch of people to see a band and was flattered to realize the cute guitarist was hitting on me. I had just agreed to head back to his 'for a drink' when a friend issued a warning.

'You don't want to go home with that guy,' she warned. 'He's known for having caveman style sex. You'll regret it.'

The comments made me laugh. A real-life caveman! However, I ignored the advice and went home with him anyway.

As soon as we got through the door my suitor made his intentions very clear. Grabbing me from behind he immediately lifted up my skirt and tore off my panties. After grappling with his jeans he took me from behind, grunting like a Neanderthal. The sex was aggressive and quick and he clearly didn't care about my experience at all. I left soon after, annoyed with myself and kind of embarrassed that my friend's warning had come true.

Tess Holliday Advice for Life #174:
Don't waste your time on sexual partners
who aren't interested in your pleasure.
Send them home to masturbate.

Tess Holliday Advice for Life #177:
Masturbation is normal and part of building a
healthy body identity. Spend time with yourself
and learn how your body responds to different
stimulation. How can you show someone how you
like to be pleasured if you can't pleasure yourself?

I would love to tell you that I learnt my lesson, that my other experiences of casual sex in Seattle were more empowering, but that would be a big fat lie. I was just not picky about who I slept with and the guys who picked me up did not care about my pleasure. Paradoxically I would go home with men because I wanted to feel desired but I would often end up leaving the situation feeling self-loathing. I allowed these guys to use me, to fuck me until they were spent, without even a thought for my own enjoyment. I was reckless with my body and my safety, rarely using protection and blindly allowing myself to be led into unknown situations.

But any attention was better than nothing, right?

Hanging out with the God gang meant that *Sex and the City*-style confessions over weekend brunch were definitely not an option. The only friend I could share my unedited sexploits with was Eddie. He had recently followed Sarah to the west coast and it was great to have him living in Seattle. Seeing my old friend doubled over laughing at my sex confessions made me wish I could be more candid with Heather. But, being a Christian, Heather was saving herself and disapproved of sex before marriage. Having her go quiet in response to my latest one-night-stand made me feel judged. I didn't want to listen to her preach about 'respecting myself'. At the time I thought Heather was being prudish, but over the years I have come to understand that it was likely more than that. I am sure it was hard for Heather to see someone she loved behaving so self-destructively. I didn't know the guys I slept with and didn't care about putting myself at risk.

Although I went to Planned Parenthood to get tested for STIs (by some small miracle I didn't have any), I ignored the advice their healthcare staff dispensed about using condoms. The guys I went home with could barely find my vagina, let alone figure out how to put a condom on. I assumed nothing bad would happen – and if it did? Well, I could die the next day being hit by a bus.

While Heather could find the silver lining with any situation and set herself high standards for how she wanted to be treated, I had more of a dark view on life. I think we clashed at times because she had not experienced much trauma in her life. She had grown up with parents who were wonderful to each other and who supported her wholeheartedly. She didn't know what it was like to go through some of the stuff I had or how it had affected me. Life kicked me in the vagina on a regular basis so why the hell should I play it safe? I had been living in Seattle for eight months when my reckless attitude finally caught up with me.

* * *

Somehow I found myself at a lame excuse for a house party, spectating as my friend Tracey got wasted. I was the bored, designated driver, nursing a warm beer and wondering when I could head home. When a guy called Chris came over to talk to me I can't say I was particularly interested, but hey, at least it killed the time.

By 1am Tracey was wasted and I had at last persuaded her to leave. When Chris and his friend offered to come along for the ride, I found myself shrugging when really

I should have just said no. I didn't care to ask where they lived or how they would subsequently get home.

Driving from one side of Seattle to the other took me a good hour and a half and by the time I dropped Tracey home it was nearing 3am. When my two additional passengers dropped the bombshell that they lived a good hour's drive back across Seattle I was not impressed.

'You can stay at mine,' I told them. 'I'll drive you home in the morning.'

Back at my apartment, Chris seemed eager to chat while his friend passed out in the living room. When he leant in to kiss me, for some reason I went with it and predictably one thing led to another. Before I knew it we were having sex in my room and, as usual, I didn't use anything. I didn't even think about it. As far as I was concerned condoms were awkward as shit – but not as awkward as childbirth.

Tess Holliday's Advice for Life #180:
Condoms. Use them. Also, get tested for STD's
regularly. Safe sex is responsible sex.

The next morning I just wanted Chris and his friend gone but I had to sit in my car making small talk for a whole hour as I drove them home. When Chris handed me his number on his way out of the car I didn't expect to see him again.

Fast-forward two weeks and I felt like I had been body-snatched. My boobs were swollen and sore and I felt weird; a raging hormone-induced kind of wired that I'd never experienced before. When my period failed to appear I began to suspect the worst.

I confided in a friend at Lane Bryant who quickly swung into action and bought me a pregnancy test. As soon as the retail day was over she marched me back to her place, escorted me upstairs to the bathroom and handed me the test.

Shutting the door, I studied the box in my hand, reluctant to face the truth. Eventually I sat on the toilet and peed on the stick. Then I waited, my pee soaked hand shaking, for my fate to be sealed. Deep down I already knew I was pregnant, but when the lines turned blue it felt like an out-of-body experience. Panic surged through me.

'Holy fuck, what do I do now?'

After crying uncontrollably in my friend's bathroom, I dejectedly drove home. All I wanted to do was talk to my mother. I stopped for gas and plucked up the courage to tell her, not wanting to prolong the inevitable.

Ironically, up until now, Mom and I had always shared a joke about me bringing shame on the family. Every phone call home I would start the conversation with, 'Hey Mom, guess what?'

To which Mom would reply: 'You're pregnant!' and we'd both laugh.

But this time there was no amusement in my voice.

'Yes, I am,' I told her quietly.

The phone went silent for a moment.

'Are you kidding me?' she said.

'No,' I replied, trying not to cry.

'Who?'

'Just some random guy.'

I don't know what I expected her to say but unsurprisingly she was pretty pissed.

'I have to go,' I told her, unable to cope with the inevitable moral lecture. Then I hung up and cried myself to sleep.

It was a few days before I called Chris and broke the news.

'You need to get an abortion,' he said.

'OK …' I replied.

I drove to his house and we had it out.

'I don't have any money,' he said, backtracking fast. 'I don't have a job.'

Next I went to Planned Parenthood where they confirmed I was pregnant and outlined my options. I hadn't ruled out an abortion but my gut feeling was that I wanted to keep the baby. Mom, being adamantly pro-life, had called me every day applying pressure. 'It's God's will to have this child,' she said.

The simple fact was no route out of this mess was easy. How would I get by as a single mom? I wanted to stay in Seattle, but how would I make that work? The anxiety of the situation was causing me sleepless nights.

Tess Holliday's Advice for Life #182:
Your body is your own. Every woman deserves the
right to choose whether or not she wants to have
a baby or not. No other argument is valid.

After living with my secret for a week I drove over to Heather's house and told her everything.

'You need to tell my parents,' she said immediately. 'They'll want to help you.'

Following Heather into the kitchen I broke the news to Steve and Rose. It was as shameful as telling my own parents but their kindness floored me.

'You're going to be OK,' Rose said, hugging me as I began to cry. 'We are here for you.'

Leaving the home of my 'Seattle parents' I definitely felt less alone. For the first time I felt optimistic that I could have a baby by myself in Seattle. I had support and I would make it work.

* * *

As far as pregnancies went mine was good. I definitely felt more tired than usual but I didn't get any morning sickness. I had a strong desire for Subway sandwiches smeared in extra mayo which seemed incredibly normal compared to some of the crazy cravings I had read about.

As I reached the four-month mark of my pregnancy I was glad to welcome Mom and Bill to Seattle for a weekend mini vacation. They had recently moved 113 miles to Canton, Mississippi, as Bill had a new job at the

Nissan plant there. After a hard few weeks getting their house ship-shape they were in need of a break. I was looking forward to taking them on a whirlwind tour of all my favorite Seattle haunts.

Their flight landed on the morning of my nineteenth birthday, and I set off for the airport full of excitement that I was going to see my mom. It was the first time I had driven to the airport and during the journey I got flustered and missed my exit to the terminal. Panicking I swung a left to change lanes just as a speeding car careered into my path. I didn't see the car until the last minute. We collided with a screeching of breaks and mangled metal and my body was jerked violently by the impact.

I stumbled out to discover that my car had been totaled. Amazingly I escaped with a fractured wrist but all I could think about was the 'what ifs' of the situation. While I had not wanted to get pregnant there was no doubt how much I cared for the life inside me. The thought of losing my baby left me shaken and I called Steve in tears. He picked me up and drove me to collect Mom and Bill who had been pacing the terminal wondering what the hell had happened.

Steve dropped us off at the hotel where the atmosphere was subdued. Feeling tired and emotionally rung out, I did not have the energy to phone round to ask a friend to drive me home. Instead I slept on the floor of the hotel room wondering how my life had once again gone to shit.

That weekend, as I showed Mom and Bill around, I tried to fake a carefree attitude. In truth, the weight of my situation was never far from my mind. What would I do without my car? How would I get to work?

'Why don't you come home to Mississippi?' Mom pleaded when the time came for her to leave. 'I can help you with the baby.'

'I don't know Mom,' I replied, stubborn to the end. 'I need to work out what I'm going to do.'

As I waved her off it pained me to see the look of concern on her face. I knew she would worry about me all the way home to Canton. Deep down I knew she was right, I should go home to Mississippi, but I couldn't quite admit it to myself. I've always been stubborn and I didn't want to give up my dreams. I had moved to Seattle to escape the South. If I headed home to be a teen mom I'd never get out!

My situation quickly went from bad to worse. With no car I had to give up my job and apartment. I crashed with my friend Chelsea and her mom in Olympia, WA for a couple of weeks and then begged Steve and Rose to take me in.

'We have friends staying,' Rose told me apologetically. 'But you could sleep in a tent in the backyard and eat meals with us?'

With no better option I agreed and pitched my camp, spending the next few nights lying in a damp tent listening to the neighboring raccoons humping (or fighting, it was hard to tell). At last I had an epiphany. What the fuck was I doing? I was almost five months pregnant and living like a vagrant – all because I was too stubborn to move back home.

Tess Holliday's Advice for Life #185:
Living in a tent while pregnant is pretty shit.

Tess Holliday's Advice for Life #188:
Pride will fuck you up every time.

Sometimes you just have to swallow your pride, take a reality check and get a grip. Did accepting help now mean my dreams were dead? Well, only if I gave up on them. I suddenly felt ashamed of myself. Yes, life was tough but I was acting like a child crying and stamping her feet because she couldn't have what she wanted when she wanted it. My life wasn't over, there were options and solutions available to me and for that I should be grateful. If I had to head back south to get back on my feet, then so be it. Seattle would still be there once I'd sorted out my mess.

The next day I put my stuff in storage and accepted my mom's offer of a plane ticket back to Mississippi.

Chapter 8

One in Six

When I abandoned my Seattle dreams to return to Mississippi it felt like I was losing my freedom. At the age of 20 I was about to become a reluctant single mother with my careless actions resulting in a life sentence of parenting.

I almost laughed when I arrived at my new home. I shit you not, the house Mom and Bill had rented in Canton cowered in the shadow of Madison County Detention Center.

Seeing the walls of a cold, uninviting prison looming over me it felt like the universe was sending me a strong message: I'd committed the crime, now I would do the time.

'Why would you want to live right next to a prison?' I asked Mom, feeling slightly freaked out that her home was barely 120 yards from the prison walls.

'It's a secure prison,' Mom replied. 'They can't do anything. Plus it's cheap and convenient for Bill's work.'

While the felons could not get near to us they could definitely see us. A few days later as I stood in the backyard to get some fresh air, I quickly realized that the inmates were out in the prison yard exercising. 'Hey baby' one yelled while another began to whistle. I quickly retreated back into the house.

While it was nice to be back with Mom I immediately noticed an atmosphere between her and Bill. She seemed subdued and not her usual positive self.

'What's up?' I asked after a week of observing terse conversations between her and my stepdad.

'Oh it's just a rough patch,' she confessed. 'Don't you worry about it.'

I suddenly realized I wasn't the only one with problems. I had dreaded moving to Canton as I knew it was small and uneventful. The town had a good flea market but that was really it. If there was a silver lining of being here, it was the fact I could offer my Mom some company and support. I could see that she was feeling isolated just like back when Dad had dragged us from place to place in my early childhood. At least now we could be miserable together!

I was well into my second trimester and feeling fairly good. While most mothers-to-be in the USA see an obstetrician from eight weeks to check on their baby's progress I was yet to have any kind of formal appointment. The simple fact was I didn't have insurance to cover maternity care and Planned Parenthood could only do so much. I had been feeling kicks in my belly for several weeks now so my gut instinct was that all was well.

I added constant cravings for my mom's (very white) Tex Mex tacos to the one for Subway sandwiches with a ton of mayo. I could eat six tacos in one sitting while binge-watching episodes of *Bad Girls Club*.

When I arrived in Canton, Mom had handed me a copy of the book *What to Expect When You're Expecting* to get me ready for the birth. Her intentions were kind but I found it far from reassuring. It basically tells you every single horrible thing that can happen during pregnancy and in my opinion it is a God-awful book. When you are already hormonal the last thing you need to read about is every gloomy scenario.

Once I had read that book I decided that I didn't need to hear any more, so when Mom suggested prenatal classes I refused. I didn't need to be traumatized any further thank you very much. It was a silly attitude really as prenatal classes can be really helpful for learning how to handle the pains of contractions.

Tess Holliday's Advice for Life #191:
You can tear from your vagina to your butthole
while giving birth. Not really advice, just thought
it might drive home the need to use birth control.

I would not advise anyone to go into a labor situation oblivious to what happens or how to handle it. When you know what is going on it is a much more empowering experience. I may have skipped the classes but I knew that I needed a prenatal check-up. Neither Mom nor I had any income to pay for healthcare but eventually I was able to organize an appointment through Medicare. I was relieved to find a really nice doctor based in Jackson, Mississippi.

'Would you like to see your baby?' the doctor asked, whipping out a tube of cold gel which he wiped on my belly with what looked like a supermarket barcode scanner.

I had never seen an ultrasound image before, and seeing my fetus for the first time was crazy. It actually looked like a baby, curled up with a cute side profile, occasionally moving its arms and legs.

The doctor turned up the monitor to reveal a rapid, urgent beating noise.

'That's the baby's heartbeat,' he said. 'It's a lot faster than yours and mine. Would you like to know the sex?'

I nodded, although I already knew I was having a girl. I just had the feeling.

'It's a boy!' he said.

I think he was expecting me to smile with delight but instead my face crumpled and I began to cry. It was kind of ridiculous seeing as I had been blessed with a healthy baby but I could not help myself. The news I was having a boy scared me. My son wouldn't have a father figure and it made me feel helpless.

'I have no idea what to do with a boy,' I cried to Mom. 'I understand how girls think, but boys? No.'

'It's going to be OK,' Mom smiled. 'You have a healthy baby and that's a blessing!'

I know now that every mom-to-be obsesses about how she will find her way with motherhood. You want to do the right thing for your child and there is nothing more daunting than knowing it is down to you to help a small, helpless human being to find their way in life and be a good person. Ultimately every mom does their best and that's all you really can do.

As it turned out, he proved to be a good, easygoing kid and the two of us have a close bond. He may not have his biological father in his life but from the age of two he has been showered with love by my ex-boyfriend John, who he calls dad to this day. He also has Nick who loves him like a son and would do anything for him. I've done my best to let him know that families all look different and that he is lucky he has two dads who adore him.

Tess Holliday's Advice for Life #199:
There are as many ways to have a functional happy family as there are stars in the sky.

Apart from my daily catcalls from a few sex-deprived felons I was yet to make any friends in Canton. Feeling stir-crazy, I borrowed Bill's car and drove 20 minutes into Jackson, Mississippi, a much bigger town, to look for work. Eventually I found a job at Hot Topic, a shop that sells alternative clothing. I vowed to work as long as I could, relishing the chance to earn some money and keep busy.

I was quickly befriended by a group of eccentric colleagues and immediately bonded with the store's gorgeous gay identical twins, Matt and Will. Will, a free spirit, who was loud and out there, shared my dark sense of humor, while Matt, who was quieter and reserved, was always full of good advice and a shoulder to cry on.

Meeting them transformed my experience of life in Canton. They made me laugh and feel as normal as a 20-year-old single mom having a baby could feel. I will always be grateful for that.

* * *

On August 29, when I was six months pregnant, the weather sirens sounded in Canton.

For days the news channels had warned us about a 'monster storm' that meteorologists were labelling the 'big one'.

Initially I wasn't worried. Growing up down south, I had heard warnings about the 'big one' hitting during hurricane season for as long as I could remember. As far as I was concerned the weathermen always erred on the side of caution. This wasn't the first time there had been hysteria about battening down the hatches. I'd heard it all before.

However, as the day wore on, I found myself questioning whether the continuing warnings could be justified this time. I had experienced plenty of hurricanes and tornadoes whipping through Mississippi but this one felt different. The storm, which had been named Hurricane Katrina, intensified after dark with the whole house shaking on its foundations. I sat with Mom in the living room, waiting for the wind to subside, but every hour it seemed to get worse and I was too anxious to try to sleep. Eventually we both knocked out on the couch, exhausted.

Around 4pm the next day morning the phone rang. It was Grandpa phoning from Laurel. 'The roof is coming off the house,' he said, before the line went dead. After that Mom could not get through at all. Not knowing what was happening to Maw and Paw was the worst and I could see Mom was struggling not to cry.

'They'll be OK,' I said, trying to keep calm even though I felt sick inside.

We sat together in the living room all afternoon and late into the night, listening to the howling winds, wondering when it would let up. Bill had gone to bed, but in the middle of the night the glass in our porch screen shattered explosively, showering the room in glass shards. Bill came dashing out to survey the damage. Within minutes the power went out. As Bill struggled to seal up the porch by torchlight, Mom and I retreated back to the living room.

'The prison has lost power,' Bill said, coming to the door with a pale face.

At any other time I would have sat there envisaging escaped rapists and murderers but all I could think about was my grandparents. They still don't even know I'm having a baby, I thought sadly. I hoped they'd made it to their storm shelter at the end of their driveway. I lay there in the flickering candlelight with my hand on my belly, silently praying to a God I wasn't sure I believed in. I could hear Mom sniffing and knew she was in tears despite her attempts to put on a brave face.

By 5am the howling began to fade and as daylight crept into the house the power began to flicker. Mom had been trying the phone all night but the line was still dead. By 7am we were able to switch the television on and I will never forget what I saw. A news channel was showing aerial footage of the Mississippi Gulf Coast. I hardly recognized it. There was flooding and devastation everywhere. Hotels, condos and stores we had been to throughout my childhood were just gone. The hurricane had even swept up a huge floating casino and dumped it unceremoniously ashore to its new home in the middle of the freeway. Then we saw footage of New Orleans and my heart just broke. There were people walking neck deep in water trying to find loved ones. It felt like a nightmare.

'We need to get to Laurel,' Mom said.

Working together we packed the car with food and blankets.

'I should stay and keep an eye on the house,' Bill said. 'There are looters everywhere.'

We set off without him, making an initial stop at the fire station in Canton where staff were handing out rations of water and ice. Laurel was only two hours' drive south of us but the journey took over four hours. The nearer we got to Laurel the more we were rerouted because of uprooted trees, snapped power poles and storm debris in the road. I shut my eyes and shuddered to think what we'd find at our destination.

Eventually we drove into Laurel. The town was a mess with fallen trees and poles all over the place. There were buildings with broken windows, collapsed walls and exposed roofs.

As we turned off the main road and drove along the debris-strewn track to my grandparents' house my heart was in my mouth.

'The pecan tree's gone,' I gasped to Mom. The roof of the house had pieces missing but seemed to be intact.

'Look!' I said, spotting two figures huddled on the porch. Maw and Paw were sleeping on mattresses under bug nets in the scorching midday heat which was already nearing 110F.

'Oh thank God,' Mom cried pulling to a stop and tumbling out of the car to embrace her parents.

'There was a tornado,' Maw said, seeming remarkably composed. 'It hit 50 feet from the house and got the pecan tree. We were in the storm shelter. We've got no power,' she added. 'The house is like an oven. That's why we're out here.'

We pulled up lawn chairs, batting away insects as Maw and Paw recalled the harrowing events of the night before. The humid aftermath of the storm meant there were thick swarms of mosquitos and love bugs – a cute name for a nuisance bug that fucks midair and is a general pain in the ass.

'Well Ryann has something to tell you,' Mom said, trying to lighten the mood.

As I confessed to being knocked up I hoped my grandparents' brush with death would make them grateful for the continuation of life. No such luck.

'Oh,' my grandmother remarked with a look of disapproval. 'Well, it's not what we wanted for you, but your grandaddy and I will support you,' she eventually added.

As we cleaned up as best we could it was clear that my grandparents could not stay at home without air conditioning. After a few hours we locked up the house and drove to Mom's sister Denise's home.

'Don will have everything under control,' Mom laughed.

Like many eccentrics in the South, my uncle Don was a 'doomsday prepper' and ready for the apocalypse. He often wore camouflage gear and had been stockpiling emergency essentials for many years. Sure enough, Don already had two emergency generators up and running when we arrived.

'Why is it so hot in here?' Mom enquired to Denise.

'He's using them to power the freezers,' she replied.

We had to laugh. There was no power to the house but Don, being a huge foodie, was determined that his perishables would not spoil. Any complaints we had soon diminished when Don produced a burner and a wok and rustled up an amazing Chinese-inspired lunch in the middle of the living room. It was one of the best meals I have ever eaten and deliciously odd in the middle of a crisis.

For the next two weeks, Mom and I remained in Laurel helping our family to clear up after the storm. It took six whole weeks for my grandparents to get their electricity back but really they got off lightly compared to so many people. Ten people were killed in Jones County alone as a result of falling trees and many agricultural businesses across the area suffered huge losses due to the damage. Thankfully we didn't know anyone who had died, but harrowing reports circulated from friends of friends about people who had been crushed or even drowned in their homes.

Ten years on I still think about Katrina and how it felt like the longest night of my life. Everyone remembers the devastation suffered in New Orleans, but in reality the destruction was much more widespread than just NOLA. So many communities along the Mississippi Gulf Coast and inland suffered too. All in all, Hurricane Katrina claimed over 1,800 lives and millions of people were left homeless as a result of the devastation.

Even now, the reminders of that day are still there and there are areas that will never be the same. As kids, Tad and I had loved going to Jazzland, a New Orleans water park, where we would spend the day hurtling down the water slides. The site was completely destroyed by the storm and no one ever cleaned it up. It sits on the horizon just off the highway, looming sadly in the distance.

* * *

As I entered the third trimester of my pregnancy my hormones went into overdrive. During one visit to my obstetrician I burst into tears.

'What if my baby is ugly?' I blurted out. 'Is my baby going to look like a swamp thing?'

While my obstetrician was well used to reassuring neurotic pregnant women, I seriously doubt he'd heard that one before.

'Do you have a history of swamp things in your family?' he asked me straight-faced.

I immediately stopped crying and laughed. 'No.'

'Then I think you will be fine,' he added with a smile.

I worked until I was about 34 weeks pregnant, but working in retail, staying on my feet, was tough. I eventually had to quit because I couldn't bend over to fold shirts.

As I reached the last few weeks of my pregnancy my appetite was out of control. Most of the local fast food vendors knew me by name and order. On January 19, everything suddenly kicked into gear. I had arrived at my doctor's office with Mom at 1pm for my last maternity check-up. As usual a nurse took my blood pressure and then my obstetrician carried out a vaginal examination.

'Good news, you're having a baby and it's happening right now!' he suddenly announced. I listened stunned as he explained that he thought my baby would likely weigh nine pounds five.

'I don't think your cervix is wide enough for the baby's head,' he added. 'I think we should do a Cesarean section.'

I was shocked but I didn't argue. With the benefit of hindsight I do sometimes still wonder if I should have asked more questions or asked for a second opinion. At this point my baby was not showing any signs of distress and my body had not been given any chance to deliver naturally. If we had waited for my contractions to start perhaps I might have had him naturally? I guess I will never know. Ultimately I trusted my doctor and was happy to go along with his advice, but the experience is yet another example of how it is always best to be well-informed and in the know.

Tess Holliday's Advice for Life #200:
Trust your instincts, and advocate for your body.

Following his instructions I went straight from my obstetrician's office to a delivery suite where I was immediately prepped for surgery. Even though I'm not shy, I was mortified when a male nurse appeared with a razor and shaved off my public hair. Ten years later, when I went in to have Bowie, I had that shit waxed in advance!

I had never been in an operating room before and I was shocked by the amount of medical staff in the room. For 20 minutes I lay terrified as nurses and doctors in scrubs flapped around me preparing for the surgery. Mom was never brought in to support me like I had been promised. I was lonely and scared and mad that she wasn't there.

When the moment came to perform the procedure I was positioned on my back with my arms spread wide like I was on a cross. Once they'd numbed my abdomen, my doctor got to work behind a screen.

'You're going to feel a strong tug now, Ryann,' my doctor said.

I felt an uncomfortable pulling sensation as he delved into my belly to pull out my baby.

'Please cry, please cry,' I prayed silently.

At 5pm I heard the beautiful sound of a squawking, angry newborn and knew my son was fine. I got a quick passing glimpse of him as the doctor whisked him away to be cleaned up.

The hardest thing was staying still while they sewed me back up. No one was talking to me and I felt upset and agitated by the thought that my baby needed me. Eventually the anesthesiologist spotted I was crying and called Mom in to calm me down. It was almost a full hour before I met my son and I found the whole experience very cold and traumatizing.

When I had Bowie it wasn't even a conversation I had to have. My obstetrician-gynecologist and the hospital believed strongly in the importance of skin-to-skin contact between mother and baby and Bowie didn't leave my side from the moment he was born. I wish I'd had the education back then to push for the same for my first son.

Finally, in a recovery room, a nurse placed my son on my chest. I held my breath struggling to believe that this adorable, little snuffling human belonged to me. He was the cutest, even if he did look like a little alien. I was relieved that he latched on right away.

Rylee Emery Hoven weighed eight pounds three, so considerably less than the giant baby I had envisaged.

'You have got a big head,' I remarked quietly, running my fingers over his warm scalp. I was relieved I hadn't pushed that melon out of my vagina.

Mom immediately bonded with Rylee and from the moment she clapped eyes on him he was her little co-conspirator. I was surprised when she informed me that my dad had made it just in time. As soon as he heard I was having the baby he had got in his car and driven for six hours to the hospital. When he finally got to see me he burst into my room with a bunch of flowers and cried with emotion when he held his first grandchild. For a naïve second it gave me hope that he might be a good grandfather.

The Cesarean left me sore and unable to sit up or lift anything, so that night my Grandma stayed at the hospital with me and helped me to feed this new strange creature.

I spent four days in hospital recovering before I could take Rylee home, but honestly I wasn't even slightly ready. I'm not sure that either me or Rylee would even be here if I'd had to do those first six weeks without Mom. I found it very hard to cope with a crying newborn and whenever Rylee started screaming I would start crying myself. Mom slept in my room and helped me with everything, but I panicked whenever I was left alone with him. I did what I needed to do. I took care of him, clothing and feeding him, but I felt like I was in a dark tunnel and some days I couldn't really see a light at the end of it. There was so much pressure on my shoulders because I didn't know what to do.

At my two week checkup I confided in my doctor.

'It sounds like you might have a bit of post-partum depression,' he said. 'Lots of new mothers feel the way you do.'

After a good talk he prescribed antidepressants, but even just having a diagnosis, even just knowing that I wasn't the only person to feel like this, really, really helped me. I left feeling like I could make this work, but in my stubborn way I was determined not to take the medication.

Tess Holliday's Advice for Life #207:
There is no shame in taking medication for your
head – it's a part of your body and no different to
taking medication for your heart or your knees.

Luckily for me Rylee was an easy baby, because I definitely was not a natural mom the first time around. I joke that he was my 'little potato'. He just lay around, taking things in, observing everything and probably secretly judging every move I made. He is still very methodical, asking a million questions before trying something; oh, and occasionally still a judgey little potato.

Amazingly he slept through the night from just a few weeks old and would sometimes take a six- or seven-hour nap during the day. Lucky little fucker.

'Is he alive?' I'd ask Mom anxiously as I hovered over the bassinet. 'Should I wake him?'

Mom would shoo me away and repeat the mantra: 'Never wake a sleeping baby!'

Rylee is still an Olympic gold medal-level sleeper. He wouldn't ever wake up before 10am if he didn't have to. During the week he hates his early morning alarm and often needs to be coaxed out of bed with the promise of his favorite breakfast – bagels with cream cheese, which he grumpily carries into the car looking like Gollum out of *Lord of the Rings*.

Being a new mom was the toughest but most rewarding thing I had ever done. The first three months passed in a fog. All I could do was take one day at a time and do my best to survive. In hindsight, I should have taken the antidepressants. There were many times I felt like my life was over and that I couldn't breathe, but Mom was always there to help me. None of my friends from Seattle had children so I couldn't really turn to them for help. They reached out in their own way, but it wasn't the same and at times I felt very isolated.

I think, like many moms, a lot of my anxiety came from losing my identity both physically and emotionally. Nothing prepares you for looking after a small, helpless human 24 hours a day. At first it feels like you will never be the same person again and, whether you are 20 or 35, that can be a terrifying and claustrophobic prospect. It really isn't unusual to feel like you have lost yourself when you become a mother. You often feel like you don't have time to focus on your body or care for yourself.

Prior to having Rylee most of my clothes had been US size 16 to 18, but post-baby I was definitely carrying some extra pounds. Buying size 20 clothes left me feeling decidedly unsexy, but I wish now that I had cut myself some slack and appreciated the incredible thing my body had just achieved.

It was Matt and Will who first reminded me that I was still a person, not just a mom. They arrived at my door to take me out to see *Brokeback Mountain* at the movies. It was strange to leave the house without Rylee but after I'd got over the initial panic of leaving my baby I started to enjoy myself. It made me realize that in order to look after my son I had to make time for myself too. There is so much pressure in America to devote your life to your kids at the expense of everything else. But while I love my boys and want to care for them I don't want to live for them. I think it is important to care for yourself so you can be there for everyone else.

Rylee was five months when I realized just how much my mom needed me.

'I'm leaving Bill,' she said. 'We're moving back to Laurel.'

The plan was for us to move out secretly and quickly while Bill was at work. She had a fear of men that was completely justified, and just wanted to avoid his wrath. My cousin Vickie worked at a moving company and helped us rent a truck. She also allocated us two of her strongest removal guys to do all the heavy lifting. My grandma looked after Rylee that day so Mom, Vickie and I could clear out our stuff.

Bill rarely came home during his lunch break but of course that day he did. He lost it and began yelling at my mom, then he turned on me.

'This is all your fault, you whore,' he spat. Thankfully we had two burly men to protect us and we finished packing up quickly and got the hell out of there. Mom bought everyone dinner at a truck stop on the way home to say thank you. We couldn't have left without those guys and I'm thankful for them every day for getting my mom out.

I had mixed feelings about moving back to Laurel. It was not where I wanted to be but it was better than Canton where I didn't have a single mom friend. I also realized I was doing pretty good by Laurel standards. A lot of people I went to school with already had three children.

I quickly got a job at Walmart, working in their portrait studio taking shots of newborn babies. It sounded fancy but actually I operated a stationary camera by pushing a button. It would always make my day to see how elaborately Walmart moms dressed their babies. My favorite shoots always featured streetwear, coordinating outfits and baby gold chains. These mothers took the shoots very seriously and would play rap or rock music on their phones to get their babes in the mood. However, I found myself lost for words when I heard a mother instruct her eight-month-old, 'You better motherfucking dance.'

Before long I had made three mom friends at the store. Rachel, who was 17 and mother to 18-month-old Allyiah; Tinisha, who, at 25, had seven kids and was pregnant with number eight, and Hannah, whose son was the same age as Rylee. Rachel and Tinisha were always there with words of encouragement, parenting tips and sound advice.

Being a mom so young meant people often looked at Rachel with pity but she was one of the most determined people I've known. When she told me she was going to college to train to be a nurse it reminded me to aim high, that being a mother didn't need to hold me back. Likewise Tinisha, with her impressive brood, had seen and heard it all. Her laidback attitude taught me not to sweat the small stuff, that every day is different as a parent and you can only do your best. I felt that Hannah was more of a fun, outrageous influence, who still went out to party, despite being a mom.

'I tell my parents I need a night to myself and drop off my kid,' she said with a glint in her eye. 'Then I go out and cut loose.'

When Rylee was nine months old Hannah invited me to join her for a night out to a club in Hattiesburg. I had been feeling lonely and was grateful for the invitation, arranging for my mom to babysit for the night. When I got into Hannah's car it never occurred to me that I didn't know her very well. I trusted her to drive to the club and then get me home again and naively headed out without a cellphone or debit cards and only a little cash.

Although the night started out well with the pair of us dancing at the club until midnight, on the way home I started to find myself out of my depth. We were driving on the freeway when two guys started trying to get our attention from a neighboring car. They gestured at us to roll down our windows. While I found this creepy Hannah seemed amused. She slowed down and rolled down the window despite me begging her not to.

'Follow us back to our place,' the driver, a chubby guy in his early twenties, shouted.

Hannah grinned back and nodded.

'Do you know them?' I asked.

'No,' she laughed, changing lanes to follow their car. Her lack of concern for the danger of the situation frightened me.

'Please don't,' I begged but she just laughed. The next thing I knew she was turning off the highway and pulling up outside an apartment building in a rundown neighborhood.

Looking back now, I should have told Hannah to kiss my fat ass and to drop me off anywhere but there, but at the time I was far too submissive. Stupidly I worried about what she would think of me for bailing so I said nothing and blindly followed her to the door of the men's apartment.

The two guys, who said they were cousins, were both drunk. After some small talk Hannah stood up and grinned at me.

'I'm leaving,' she said. 'I'll be back in 20 minutes.' What the fuck! Panicked I followed her outside.

'I'm coming with you,' I insisted.

'No, you're not,' she said firmly, a look of irritation flashing across her face. 'Stay and I will be back soon.'

To this day I don't know why I let her leave me there. Feeling confused and scared, I walked back into the apartment to find both men looking at me knowingly.

'My cousin wants to have sex with you,' the chubby guy said.

I laughed nervously. He had to be kidding.

'So you're gonna have sex with him and if you don't,' he paused, his face cold and devoid of any emotion, 'then you have to have sex with both of us.'

My eyes welled with tears and I felt a lump in my throat. The inevitability of where this situation was going hit me and my eyes darted to the door. The two guys were watching me, reminding me of lions stalking their prey, and I knew if I tried to run the situation could get a whole lot worse. Silently trembling with fear, I followed the tall guy into the other room where he pushed me down on the bed. He took my clothes off and I lay there while he forced himself on me, into me, trying not to scream from the pain. I mentally checked out – I just wanted him to finish so it would be over.

After what seemed like an eternity he passed out on top of me. I lay there, too scared to move a muscle, hurting and terrified, contemplating what I should do. I had to get out of there. He weighed a ton but summoning every ounce of strength I had, I managed to roll him off me and slid quietly off the bed. After dressing quickly I peered around the door. The coast was clear. Quietly I grabbed my rapists phone and tried to call my mom but the call wouldn't connect.

With tears streaming down my face and my heart in my mouth I tip-toed out of the apartment. I don't even know if I shut the door behind me but I remember once I got out the night air hit me in the face and I gasped to breathe. I started to run, but my body was sore and I felt nauseous from the trauma so I slowed to a walk. I don't know how long I walked for, or where I thought I was going but I just kept walking. After what seemed like forever, I saw Hannah's car. She pulled up beside me and stopped.

'Did you get you some?' she said rolling down the window.

I just quietly got in the car, knowing she was my only hope of getting home. As she started to drive us back to Laurel she told me gleefully how she had left to have sex with a guy at the University of Southern Mississippi.

'Don't be sad, you know you liked it!' she told me as she dropped me home.

As she waved me goodbye like nothing had happened all I could think about was how much I hated her for leaving me.

The next morning I woke up and vomited. It also burnt when I peed, which I put down to the rough way he had forced himself into me. But throughout the day my temperature soared and by early evening I was hallucinating. Mom found me on the bathroom floor vomiting from the pain.

'I think I need to go to the ER,' I weakly told her.

I couldn't bear to tell her the truth so instead I told her I'd had sex with a guy I had a crush on and that he must have given me something. It was definitely not what she wanted to hear from her daughter but we strapped Rylee into his car seat and she drove me to the local hospital.

Several hours later I was embarrassed to be diagnosed with three sexually transmitted diseases: gonorrhea, chlamydia and trichomoniasis. Thankfully all three are treatable. It's a small grace that he didn't give me anything incurable. Ultimately I was able to get rid of all three infections, but it really fucked me up mentally for a long time. The whole experience made me understand why so many women don't speak up about being raped. I always pictured rape to be violent and unexpected, a situation where a woman is dragged into an alleyway and attacked. I think that is the scenario that people find the easiest to sympathize with. But now, I know that there are so many grey areas. Did I make a mistake trusting Hannah that night? Yes. Did I deserve to be forced to have sex? Absolutely not. It took me a long time to really admit to myself that I had been raped, because at the time I felt I'd 'let him' do it.

Tess Holliday's Advice for Life #209:
No matter what you did, no matter what you
wore, how you acted, or what situation you
put yourself in, rape is never your fault.

Sadly my rape was a dirty little secret I kept to myself until I began to understand there should be no shame. Technically I didn't tell my rapist no, but I sure as hell didn't consent. I let him assault me because I was afraid of what would happen if I didn't. I wish I had spoken up and got help because it traumatized me for a long time.

It's been ten years since I was raped and it still affects me sometimes. But talking about it helps. I am no longer embarrassed or ashamed. I know it wasn't my fault.

According to RAINN.org, one in six women in America have experienced rape in their lifetime. That's over fifty-three million women. That figure fills me with dismay and fear for the next generation, especially when we see prominent public figures failing to be held accountable for sexual assault. We have talked with Rylee about consent. He knows to keep his hands to himself and not to touch people without permission. Bowie is already learning the same concepts. And when they are interested in girlfriends (or boyfriends, or both, or neither – no judgement from us) we will make sure that they understand consent isn't silent and it isn't optional.

Chapter 9

$700 and a Pack 'n Play

Whenever I was having a Fuck My Life moment or feeling hopeless I turned my thoughts to Rylee. Whatever life threw at me, whatever crap went down, he was my reason for carrying on. A mere glimpse of his happy face and outstretched arms as he tried to scale the crib to get to me each morning filled me with joy, love and hope for the future.

I've made a lot of mistakes in my life (and I am sure there are many more to come) but caring for my children has always given me purpose. Bringing two beautiful boys into this world is the achievement I am most proud of.

Rylee's first year flew by, as it always does, with my 'little nugget' growing from a laidback, thoughtful baby to a funny, happy toddler. Watching my son's tenacity in reaching his milestones, whether that be crawling, wobbly attempts to walk or his determination to fight me for the television remote control, was a reminder to keep challenging myself. Babies and toddlers are fearless when it comes to attempting the insurmountable. Nothing holds them back. I think we could all do with a dose of that confidence later in life as insecurity and doubts set in. Like all mothers who beat themselves up, those moments were frequent for me. I can tell you now that nothing makes a single mom feel more dejected than hearing the name 'Dada' as her one of her son's first words.

Of all the words I had been encouraging Rylee to say, 'Dada' was not on the list. I didn't believe it when I heard it once, but then when he said it again and again I felt bemused and a little sad. If only I had known that babies typically say 'Dada' first because 'Da' is one of the first sounds they can master. I beat myself up for a while over that one, although now I can see the funny side.

As Rylee's first birthday approached I went all out.

I spent weeks planning a lavish party with a dinosaur theme to be held at our home in Laurel and invited all my friends and family. No expense was spared as I ordered fancy customized invitations and commissioned two cakes – a small 'smash' cake for Rylee to destroy and a big one for the party.

On the day Mom and I worked tirelessly to decorate the house with green, yellow and blue streamers and balloons and first birthday banners. It was all a bit over the top and the future kids' parties I organized were definitely more modest. I think most mothers will admit that first birthdays are really for the parents because the baby has no clue what is happening and often misses half the celebration because they are napping.

The amount of gifts Rylee received was obscene but of course he could not have cared less. It was the boxes and wrapping paper that got him drooling. He could not get enough of them.

The party went really well with everyone dear to us making a special effort to join the celebration. I was especially touched that my dad drove over from Alabama for the party laden with gifts for his grandson. Sadly it was the first and last party for Rylee he ever attended. He has never acknowledged a birthday since – not mine, or either of my sons.

It pains me to say this was really the beginning of the end for our relationship as Dad's efforts to be a father or grandfather faded. I saw him one further time a few months later when I drove to Woodstock, Alabama, but after that I grew tired of the one-way effort. When I moved out of state again I realized Dad's attitude was largely 'out of sight, out of mind'. He never once offered to visit me on the West coast or even in Laurel when I returned to visit family. Although it hurt to acknowledge that my father could so easily forget his 'old' family it was not really a great surprise. If there's one thing I can rely on, it is the knowledge that I can't rely on my Dad.

While I enjoyed living with Mom and being close to my grandparents, Laurel was beginning to break my spirit. I would often daydream about my short stint in Seattle. I could not reverse the way that moving to the West coast had opened my eyes. It had made me acutely aware that plenty of the people I met every day had no interest in the world outside of where we lived. Ignorance was bliss in their little bubble. Thinking back to how naïve I had been before I moved to Seattle the last thing I wanted was to raise my son in a place where many were content to ignore science. I was determined that Rylee was going to learn all about dinosaurs and cavemen and he would not be schooled in Laurel.

Working over 50 hours a week at Walmart was beginning to feel like drudgery. My job was repetitive and not particularly challenging. I could feel my drive and ambition ebbing away with every shift. My enthusiasm was dampened even further whenever I saw Hannah. Just a glimpse of her across the store took me back to that awful night and I would feel sick to my stomach.

I spent my breaks at work in the store's Subway franchise plotting my return to Seattle. Could I set up a life there with Rylee? I knew it would not be easy but I was sure I could find a better job. Surely there would be opportunities for me to work as a make-up artist in Seattle? The place was a hotbed of creativity.

Making the decision to leave Laurel was painful. After everything Mom had been through with Bill I knew that spending time with Rylee had got her through some difficult months. Rylee doted on his 'Nonna' and they were thick as thieves. The last thing I wanted to do was hurt Mom, so for a while I saved my money and made plans in secret. Heather promised to spread the word of my imminent return and soon I had arranged to rent a room with a mutual friend Kendra. After scrimping and saving I paid the first month's rent up front. Then I bought plane tickets for Rylee and me. With our fate sealed I finally broke the news to Mom. As I feared she took it badly.

'You're taking Rylee away from me,' she said. 'I'll never get to see him.'

She was so mad that she refused to talk to me. It sucked but I had made up my mind.

'I want to make something of myself for Rylee,' I reasoned. 'I have to do this.'

The day before the move Heather flew in to help. I had whittled down our belongings to the bare essentials, which I had crammed into three suitcases. I also had a car seat and a Pack 'n Play travel crib for Rylee. Everything else I put into storage.

When the time came for us to leave I was sad to see Mom had left for the day and would not answer her phone. I hoped that she would eventually come round and visit us in Seattle.

As Heather, Rylee and I boarded the plane in New Orleans a familiar feeling of excitement and fear hit me.

'Here I go again,' I thought. Only the stakes were so much higher this time. I had Rylee to think about. Undoubtedly I had a hard task ahead of me. I had no job nor any possible leads for one, no car, not much money and not much of a plan. But what I did have was determination.

'You just have to be positive,' Heather said, helping to ease my frantic mind. 'Things will fall into place and whatever happens you will make it work.'

* * *

My new home was in Greenwood, Seattle, an up-and-coming neighborhood that was still affordable. Introducing a toddler into our living space was challenging. Kendra, was your usual fun-loving 20-something who was in a band called the Snot Rockettes and lived a carefree life without responsibility. The apartment was far from baby-proofed.

Then there was Kendra's live-in pet hedgehog, Blanka. When Rylee saw him, his eyes nearly popped out his head. Suddenly it was his life's ambition to touch him. Unsurprisingly, being loomed upon by a clumsy toddler was alarming for Blanka who would bare his quills whenever Rylee came near. I'd have to manhandle Rylee away who would scream at the injustice of the situation. Then, no matter how hard I scoured the floor for discarded quills, a crawling Rylee would magically find them and I was constantly pulling them out of his hands.

Having arrived in Seattle with just $700 to my name, I was feeling a lot of pressure to find a job and get set up. This was my second time coming to Seattle to make it work and I felt like it was make or break. I wanted to change my life and be serious about it. I wanted to succeed and prove that I wasn't a loser.

While my friends were always out enjoying life (just as you should in your early twenties) my circumstances and responsibilities had changed dramatically. None of my social circle had kids so I was finding my feet as a young single mother without any friends with shared experience to lean on.

In time, I did find other moms who imparted words of wisdom, invaluable tips or who were just able to empathize about how hard it gets. It really is not a cliché that it 'takes a village to raise a child'. Bringing up kids never stops being challenging and I don't think a week goes by without me reaching out either by Facebook or a text to a mom friend for their take on things. That's why I am so vocal on social media about the trials and tribulations of raising small humans. Pretending everything is perfect, or mom-shaming other parents helps no one. Having children is the most rewarding experience in the world and it is also one of the hardest.

During those first few uncertain weeks I was able to supplement my paltry savings with help from the government. People can be very scathing about 'welfare moms' on food stamps but being offered just a small bit of help was the lifeline I needed to provide for my child and better my life. A case worker I was allocated through the Department of Social Services helped me find a job.

My new position was working as a teller at Washington Mutual bank. Once again, I was able to take that job and afford daycare for Rylee because the government subsidizes childcare fees for low income earners. When I hear people complaining about government 'freeloaders' I always tell them how being on welfare was my first step to being a financially independent parent. I would not be where I am now without that help.

Juggling a full-time job with being a single mom was not easy. Every morning I would walk Rylee ten blocks to daycare and then commute to the bank via bus. In the afternoon I'd have to rush to catch the bus back to pick up Rylee before his daycare closed, all the while contemplating what I should give him for dinner.

With no car we went just about everywhere via public transport, which is never simple with a small child. One day as I carried Rylee through shin-high snow to catch our bus I slipped, dropping him and landing in a heap myself. Rylee's fall was broken by the snow and he was none the worse for wear but when I looked up at the bus I saw people laughing. Cradling my crying toddler I made a second attempt to get to the bus only to have the driver slam the door shut and drive off. The lack of compassion from all concerned left me sobbing at the bus stop.

I had a ton of moments like that, which made me wonder if I had made the right choice. I often felt like I didn't know what I was doing and had bitten off more than I could chew. Thankfully Mom had finally forgiven me for 'deserting' her and was always just a phone call away.

'Just hang on in there,' she told me when I called in tears. 'It will get better.'

She was right. The shitty moments were definitely countered by kind gestures from friends who often drove me to the store or offered to babysit so I could have a break. Then there were the magical visits to Heather's home across town where Rose and Steve showered Rylee with love and gave us whatever they could. Often Rose had saved a bunch of discounted groceries which helped save my ass so many times.

* * *

Day to day, I enjoyed my job at the bank and got along with my customers who were soon greeting me by name and even brought in small gifts for Rylee. As my confidence grew, I began to feel more like my old self, enjoying the work and grown-up interactions. I think most mothers will understand that feeling of losing your identity when you have a child. You become so conditioned to putting your baby's needs first and worrying about their wellbeing that you almost lose yourself.

Like most new moms, any commitment I had to personal style had fallen by the wayside after Rylee's birth but little by little I was reviving it. I started by having my septum pierced and added a Kewpie doll tattoo on my left leg with the *Dirty Dancing* quote, 'Nobody puts baby in a corner' – a favorite of my mom's. Later I had a collection of make-up brushes, lipstick and other items you'd generally find rolling around the bottom of a handbag added to my left arm to divert attention away from the coffin monstrosity.

When you're planning to get a tattoo there are always people who comment, 'What if you regret it in ten years' time? What will it look like when you are old?' Ignore those people. Those people are motivated by fear. Do I still think it's funny to tell the story of how I was eating a packet of Hello Kitty gummies and decided on a whim to get a cartoon cat on my ankle? Yes, yes I do.

Tess Holliday's Advice for Life #212:
Don't limit yourself because you're scared
of looking stupid. It's liberating to just
embrace your inner dork.

While I covered up my tattoos for work at the bank, I wore them with pride in my own time, throwing off my cardigans for the very first time. Just like the lady I'd met in Lane Bryant, I too was attracting admiring glances from strangers. I was starting to learn to love my body, and it showed in how others responded to my new-found confidence. I was always so proud when someone stopped me in the street to comment 'Beautiful artwork!'

With the confidence boost that my new tattoos helped instill in me, I embarked on my first ever shoot with actual hair and make-up. It fell into my lap through my friendship with an art photographer I had met named Elizabeth Raab.

We were seeing a band at a local bar when she suggested that she shoot me. I loved that her work was full of rich, dark colors but she mostly shot nudity, which at the time was something that absolutely terrified me. Sure enough, she pitched me the concept: plus-size women in warrior poses ... but nude!

The days leading up to the shoot I was terrified, I had real hair and make-up and even though she knew I wasn't a model, I felt an immense amount of pressure to give her something amazing. On the day of the shoot, I met them at the location which was in Pioneer Square, in a Persian rug store her friend owned.

I got into hair and make-up while she set up the lights and got the set ready, I remember feeling so sick to my stomach, but I tried my best to not let it show. The make-up artist put in luscious extensions and braided my hair well past my ample ass. My make-up made me feel so beautiful that I didn't want to ever wash my face. I was fully nude with sheer, jewel-toned fabric draping my pale, fat body. I was so hyper aware that my breasts pointed down and the way that the fabric clung to my fat rolls. I felt like the room of three people were thinking I shouldn't be there, despite their energy and words saying otherwise; they were so supportive. I felt so powerful, but so fragile ... and also very exposed. The store front was on a street and people were walking by staring at me while I held two vintage swords aloft in my hands as I sat surrounded by Persian rugs with my tits out.

After about the fifth drunk man stumbled by sticking his face to the glass and trying to get a look at me, I jokingly asked Elizabeth to take her shirt off too to make me more comfortable. She smiled at me, and with a flick of her beautiful long black hair, she said, 'I will if that will make you feel better!' Without missing a beat she tore her shirt off and started shooting me, topless.

The nerves disappeared and I put my strongest MySpace-honed selfie face forward. To this day, it's one of my favorite shoots, and my first truly empowering moment as a model. She was honestly way ahead of her time. The photo now hangs in my house as a reminder of where I started and the day I started to unknowingly love the skin I'm in.

Other than this experience, my dreams of modeling were put on the backburner so I could dedicate my spare time away from the bank to getting more experience as a make-up artist. I had begun to pick up some work providing make-up at weddings, photoshoots and even a charity catwalk show.

Life was good – until it gave me another boot to the fupa.

When the subprime mortgage disaster hit the USA in 2008 the banking world plummeted into turmoil. For weeks I witnessed my colleagues talking in hushed tones about how Washington Mutual was struggling. I didn't want to believe the rumors so mostly I chose to ignore it and hope for the best.

In October 2008 I returned from a week-long vacation to visit Mom in Mississippi to the news my branch was closing immediately. I was devastated and scared. I had been in my job for ten months and Rylee and I had recently moved out of Kendra's place into a new one-bedroomed apartment. I had rent to pay and a child to support. What would I do now?

After a week of filling in social security paperwork and scanning recruitment websites, I was offered a lifeline. My old boss had moved to Credit Union, a smaller bank about ten blocks from Washington Mutual.

'I think you're a good worker,' she said. 'I want to offer you a job as a cashier.'

I started the following week.

* * *

After my horrific experience in Laurel it was hard for me to trust men. But I was also lonely and wanted someone in my life. I decided to give internet dating a try.

At first I was not very impressed. For some reason I kept getting matched with guys in the military or preachers. I mean, it was a Christian dating site, but I couldn't help but feel like these men were no better than the slack-jawed Christian yokels my mother had tried to get me interested in back home.

Reluctantly I agreed to a date with a youth minister. As soon as I met him at a coffee shop I regretted my decision. We were as different as chalk and cheese and had nothing to say to each other.

My next internet date with a former soldier was even less promising.

'I'm sorry, I have to breathe into this to prove I have no alcohol in my blood,' my date explained as he puffed into a tube attached to his truck dashboard. 'I got busted for driving under the influence.'

He made it sound like it had happened just the once but who gets a mandatory alcohol breath test installed in their car after 'one' DUI? He was clearly a serial offender and I was not impressed.

I decided to give him a chance but things went from bad to worse. I mean, of course they did! The guy did not ask me a single question about myself and could not hide his disinterest at being on a date with me. He was hardly a catch himself with his driving convictions.

Another guy took me to a cheap taco joint and then got mad because I wanted water instead of soda with my four-dollar combo meal. He even argued with the staff, who would not give him a discount, leaving me wishing the ground would swallow me up.

On our next date he unleashed hell on an inanimate object – the flypaper hanging in my apartment.

'That is fucking disgusting,' he ranted, the veins in his forehead bulging as he eyeballed the dangling sticky tape I'd hoped would catch an invasion of fruit flies. It was as if he'd walked into my apartment to find 50 feral cats shitting everywhere.

There was no date three.

In hindsight, I'm embarrassed that I granted this discourteous man a second date at all. The fact is I felt guilty for being a single mom and was determined to commit to dating until I found Rylee a suitable father figure. That is until I realized that you don't *need* a dude in your child's life, especially not a boring tightwad with anger issues. Sorry, let me breathe into your breathalyzer so we can drive because YOU'RE OBVIOUSLY SUCH A CATCH.

Tess Holliday's Advice for Life #219:
Never settle because you feel like you won't
find better. You will. You're worth the wait.

It is amazing I stayed online at all, but eventually I got talking to someone refreshingly normal.

At 31, John was nine years older than me but I did not mind the age gap. I liked that he had an open face with a nice smile and pretty eyes. There was a kindness to him and he was intelligent and straightforward. Too many people on dating websites want to talk about themselves or be validated by your attention but John was not like that. After my bad dating experiences I wanted to be with someone who was responsible and steady and that was John for sure.

We hit it off immediately, chatting about Tiki culture, silent films, monster movies and books. He told me that he had just started working as a teacher and had two masters from film school. The only problem was John lived in Los Angeles – 1,135 miles from Seattle.

For the next few weeks I messaged John every day while working at the bank. I confided in him that I was a single mom still trying to figure my life out.

'I don't like my new job,' I admitted one day, while quickly checking no staff members were lurking behind me. 'My old bank was a lot more fun to work at.'

'What would you like to do?' he asked. I told him about my plus size modeling and ambition to become a special effects make-up artist. I was still picking up clients as a self-taught make-up artist but had been experimenting recently with more dramatic looks. It was so easy to confide in John and soon we were chatting on Skype as well after Rylee had gone to bed. In a short space of time I'd got to know him well and now I was curious to meet him.

After speaking to John for a month I decided to bite the bullet. I arranged for a friend to care for Rylee for the weekend and bought a flight to LA. A small part of me did wonder what I was doing as the plane hurtled towards California.

'If he's a weirdo I'll turn around and get on the first plane back to Seattle,' I told myself.

John wasn't a weirdo. As soon as I saw him waiting for me in arrivals with that same calm, warm smile I felt at ease.

John lived with his grandparents so had promised to get us a room for the weekend. Well, I think in my head I had built up this romantic fantasy of staying in a fancy hotel with a plush suite, room service and huge, fluffy towels – basically the Beverly Wilshire, aka *Pretty Woman*. So I was kind of disappointed when we ended up in a cheap, dreary motel room behind a parking lot in east LA. I realized later that John was being practical rather than cheap. He had simply booked a hotel near to where his family lived and that was that.

I swallowed my disappointment and called Mom to let her know I had arrived safely. Meanwhile, John lay down on the bed and closed his eyes. By the time my call was finished he was sound asleep. I hoped it was just a catnap but John slept for a full four hours! I passed the time watching TV and going on Facebook, swinging from mild amusement at his laidback attitude and frustrated irritation.

Well, that first day kind of set the tone for our relationship. After that it was steady and comfortable but never really romantic or passionate. I do believe that the way a man kisses you is an indicator of what he is like in bed, and if I'm honest our first kiss was pretty lackluster. When John pressed his lips on mine there was no urgency, he didn't even pucker them. Any child of my generation would know what I'd learnt as a tween from the Disney film *The Little Mermaid*. Sebastian the Crab instructed Ariel: 'You gotta pucker your lips like dis!'

When we slept together it was nice but I'm not sure we made the earth move.

'You can't have it all,' I told myself. What really mattered was that John was a good guy and I liked spending time with him.

The next time we met, John flew to Seattle where he met Rylee for the first time.

During our many online chats John had told me candidly that he didn't want to have children, so I wondered how the weekend would pan out. Rylee was a crazy two-year-old with endless energy but the two of them hit it off immediately.

It was hard to get Rylee to sit still for even a minute, but to my surprise he clambered on to John's lap to read a storybook. For someone who didn't want kids John was a natural. He pulled faces making Rylee laugh and sat on the floor building brick towers with him.

After that Rylee was often the third wheel on our dates. John loved spending time with him and was always thinking of new and imaginative ways to entertain him. It warmed my heart to see them together. I realized I had fallen on my feet to find a man who was so wonderful to my son.

* * *

Speaking to John each day helped break up the monotony of my days at work. So far I had failed to bond with my new work colleagues, who handed me the crappiest chores. Suddenly it was down to me to sign hundreds of holiday cards for our customers because another member of staff who was a Jehovah Witness said it was against his 'religious beliefs'.

'I'm also a Jehovah Witness,' I told my boss petulantly when the task was passed on to me. She made me do it anyway, as my 'highly religious' colleague watched on, smiling and winking at me smugly.

Another workmate was extremely emotional and always crying in the staff bathroom. One day I was talking to a banker when she burst into the room and interrupted our conversation.

'Shut your face,' the banker barked. 'Grown folks are talking.'

She looked like someone had punched her in the face and quickly left the room. I burst out laughing, which admittedly was not the kindest of responses, and at no point did I attempt to console her in the bathroom.

Well, guess what? Karma got me. I complained loudly about lots of things at work until three months into the job I was fired. I did not have a job but I did have a new favorite slur, which I have since gifted to Nick. 'Shut your face, grown folks are talking' is now our family insult of choice.

My next job was working as a receptionist for a dentist called Dr Hsu.

My working life was now ruled by Dr Hsu's assistant – a terrifying woman. She would not let me take lunch and was ruthlessly self-sufficient and unhelpful. It was my job to schedule the appointments and optimize my boss's time. This was easier said than done. I had no clue how long a root canal or crown would take and my colleague was not about to enlighten me.

'Oh you'll figure it out,' she shrugged coldly. I could tell she was secretly enjoying every scheduling mistake I made – especially when Dr Hsu shouted at me.

Eventually she left to take another job and things began to improve. By now I had taught myself everything I needed to know about being a dentist's receptionist, including how our billing worked. I was staggered to discover that my former colleague had been billing for many services incorrectly and Dr Hsu was owed in the region of $20,000. My diligence won me favor with my employer who gave me a raise. I still had to skip lunch but Dr Hsu's attitude towards me had changed dramatically. He would often bring me Asian delicacies to eat at my desk and even drove me to Rylee's daycare if I'd got stuck on a call and missed my bus.

Life was hectic, as I juggled time for Rylee, John and my make-up jobs, but my dreams of modeling were still there in the back of my mind. One quiet morning in the office I joined up to a social networking site called Model Mayhem and uploaded some photos from a recent shoot I'd done with a friend. I gave myself the profile name Tess Typhoon, as it was kitschy and fun and befitting of an alternative model.

* * *

I had been working at Dr Hsu's office for eight months when John asked me to move to Los Angeles. It was a big ask. I loved Seattle and as far as I was concerned LA paled in comparison. But I also knew there was no chance of John relocating, not when he had a good job and family in LA. We had been dating long-distance since the start of 2008 and one of us had to make the sacrifice.

'Give LA a chance,' John reasoned. 'I'll make you fall in love with it.'

It wasn't an easy decision but ultimately I wanted to take a chance on John. The way I see it, if you think a person is worth it, you have to be willing to try.

Tess Holliday's Advice for Life #222:
You're doing yourself a disservice if you don't
pursue every option, even the difficult ones.

Chapter 10

Heavy

It's strange how things work out. I never imagined in a million years that I would end up in Los Angeles. LA has been my home for eight years and even now I still have a love/hate relationship with the city and sometimes wonder how I got here.

It was in December 2009 that I took a chance on love and moved away from the one city that truly felt like my home. I was prepared to make the leap because I thought John might be 'the one' (um, spoiler alert – he obviously wasn't). Despite the way things turned out, it was one of the best decisions of my life.

Tess Holliday's Advice for Life #245:
Take a chance on love, no matter how
ridiculous it seems. What do you have to lose?

So I packed up my belongings and sold what I could. It was hard leaving a good job behind, especially when Dr Hsu begged me not to go. He finally sent me on my way with a $2,000 farewell bonus. That extra cash helped us no end during those first few months in California and I will always be grateful.

Compared to Seattle, LA was brash, noisy and polluted. I hated the congested five-lane highways and the hustle and bustle, but I loved John so I tried not to complain. The hardest thing was giving up my independence and needing to rely on John and his family. In Seattle I could walk or take a bus to most places but LA is not a pedestrian-friendly place. The city is so spread out that you need a car to get around so suddenly I was relying on John to drive me or lend me his car.

Then there was the unfamiliarity of moving into John's grandparents' home in east LA. But to my relief, Martha and Abelardo loved Rylee and treated him like one of their own. They had raised John and four of his siblings after his mom and dad divorced so were used to having kids around. Needless to say I often worried he was getting under their feet or that I was asking too much of them. Especially as they cared for him when he was home from preschool and I was out at work.

At first my job hunt did not go smoothly. The first two dental offices I found work at were shady. I suspected they were taking people's money for treatment they didn't need and I had no desire to be complicit. Despairing, I called Dr Hsu.

'You need to look for a family owned business that takes PPO insurance,' he told me. 'That way you know it will be legitimate.'

I took his advice and got a job at a small family practice in San Dimas, a city about 30 miles from east LA. I worked for two dentists: Dr Jeong Monday to Wednesday and his niece, Dr Foon, on Thursdays and Fridays. Everything seemed above board and the office was pleasant – even though my colleagues constantly watched Fox News.

Living with John in LA was steady. We quickly eased into family life spending our weekends going out to eat, visiting museums or seeing movies. John continued to be wonderful with Rylee, who had just turned three, always thinking of fun things for them to do together. In the evenings he would encourage Rylee to read to him or scrabble around on the floor building towering struc- tures out of Lego. It warmed my heart to see how much Rylee adored and looked up to him. John was exactly the father figure my little boy needed.

One Saturday, as we drove through LA to a beach clean-up day, Rylee surprised John with a question.

'John, can I call you Dad?' he chirped from the backseat.

'Of course you can,' John replied. There was no hesi- tation on John's part. He was thrilled and is an amazing father to Rylee to this day.

* * *

I had been in LA for a few months when I asked Nikko Hurtado, a now world famous tattoo artist, to add Mae West's face to my right arm. John had a Charlie Chaplin tattoo done by him and as soon as I saw how amazing it was I started dreaming of all the things I would like him to adorn my body with. I settled on Mae West being first because she is basically the original Hollywood badass femme. When it comes to blonde bombshells everyone always thinks about Marilyn Monroe, but Mae definitely paved the way for her. Mae might not have been considered conventionally beautiful but to me she is stunning and absolutely embodies feminism, being unapologetically sexy and pushing boundaries in a time where women were expected to be demure in life and on screen. In 1927 she was jailed for ten days on obscenity charges relating to her Broadway production '*Sex*' – and if reports are to be believed she wore silk underwear the entire time. What a woman!

Miss Piggy was next – she might be made out of felt but she was one of the only fierce fat femmes that I was exposed to in my young life. This set the tone for my right arm becoming a gallery of empowering femme icons. Dolly was next – I feel like I popped out of the womb holding a can of hairspray, and I've always loved an excessive amount of cleavage. Drag icon Divine rounds out the current selection, if you aren't familiar with her work in John Waters films then you need to put down this book and go watch every one you can get your hands on. *Female Trouble* is my personal favorite.

Tess Holliday's Advice for Life #253:
Surround yourself with symbols and people
that empower you. Or if you're like me,
use your big fat body as a big fat canvas.

'Why don't you get one of me?' Mom suggested.

'Because I don't want to look at you when I'm having sex,' I replied.

Before long I had also added artwork to the back of my legs in celebration of my grandparents. My left leg has the word 'Paw' with cowboy boots, a hat and an old oil rig for my grandpa who worked in the oil industry. On the right is a hummingbird, a diamond and a box of chocolates with the word 'Maw'. This is my tribute to my grandma's old school glamour. It represents the happy memories I have of scouring the house for hidden chocolates and the joy of sitting watching hummingbirds flit around the 20-odd feeders in her backyard.

Despite my expanding tattoo collection I entered a model search competition for plus size fashion brand Torrid. When I had finished my application I decided to log on to Model Mayhem for the first time in about a year. I was dismayed by what I found – an inbox packed full of messages from pervy guys. The messages ranged from, 'Can I shoot naked photos of you?' to 'You're hot. Let's have sex.' Then there were the messages from the fat fetish guys who wanted to 'feed me'. Ugh! I was about to delete the lot when I noticed a message that seemed less creepy. It had been sent that very day by a woman claiming to be a casting director.

'I'd like you to come in for an audition,' she wrote. 'It's for a new TV show and I think you'd be great for it.'

She had instructed me to email her outside of the site and set up an audition time. I immediately Googled the production company to check it was genuine. It was! Their office was based at the swanky CNN building on Sunset Boulevard. Feeling excited I emailed her and set up a time for an audition.

A week later I was ushered into a small studio and positioned in front of a camera.

'Hi Tess,' the producer greeted me. I was confused for a second then remembered the pseudonym I had written on my call sheet.

'My name's actually Ryann,' I admitted.

'Oh, that's OK, we like Tess better,' she said bluntly. Then she began to bombard me with questions: 'What is your experience of being overweight? Have you had any negative experiences? Have you ever been bullied? How did that make you feel?'

'Um, not great,' I answered, wondering what the point of all this was. I managed to add a few sentences about learning to love myself before she ushered me out the door again and marched me towards the elevator.

'Hey, are you based in LA?' she called out as the doors began to close.

'Yes, I am,' I replied.

'OK, good to know.'

'That was pretty fucking weird,' I told John. I had insisted he wait outside in case it was all a big scam.

I didn't know what to expect but soon after an email arrived from the producer. I thought it would tell me if I'd got the job, but no such luck.

'Our production company also films *Biggest Loser*,' the email read. 'Would you like to go on the show?'

My heart fell. *Biggest Loser* was a show that encouraged fat people to compete to lose weight. I had never liked it as I felt it exploited fat people and humiliated the contests by making them do embarrassing challenges.

'I'm sorry, but no,' I replied.

Tess Holliday's Advice for Life #259:
Authenticity is important. Never do anything
that isn't in line with your personal ideals and
morals, not matter how good the money is.

I was in a bit of a funk but then I received some amazing news. I'd made the top 25 for Torrid's model search and would compete with the other finalists for votes. All the finalists' photographs were featured on *Torrid's* Facebook page and I needed to get enough votes to make the top six.

Sadly it was not the fun experience I had expected. Every photo had accumulated comments and I was shocked to see that some of mine were critical! There seemed to be a lot of anger directed towards Torrid for not picking bigger plus size models. Naively I'd assumed the plus size community would be loving and supportive, but at size 20 I was being body shamed for not being not big enough!

'But we're all plus sized and curvy,' I replied.

This was really my first introduction to how unpredictable and volatile social media can be. You do your best but you can never please everyone.

Tess Holliday's Advice for Life #261:
People will say things online that they would
never say to your face. Console yourself with
the fact that it's usually a projection of how they
feel about themselves. You can still tell them
to eat a bag of dicks though.

I didn't make the final six in the Torrid model competition but my disappointment was short-lived. The same day the producer from my casting call phoned.

'We'd really like you to be the face of the show we're producing. Congratulations! If you want it, you've got the job!' she said. 'We'll be in touch with the details.'

My mind was spinning. I'd just got my first professional modeling job!

On a warm fall day I arrived at Sirens Studio on Sunset Boulevard. I had agreed to a fee of $2,000 for two shoots but still didn't know the details of the show.

'You're going to be the face of an A&E show called *Heavy*,' a female producer finally revealed. 'It's a mini documentary that follows people's weight-loss journeys.'

My initial reaction was to feel conflicted. I had spent the last month canvassing for votes as a plus-size woman embracing her curves. Could I really agree to be the face of a weight-loss show as well? But once I saw some footage I felt much better about it. The show may have been about weight loss, but it was following the people's journeys in an interesting and sensitive way.

With my mind at ease I followed the producer to hair and make-up where she introduced me to the crew of professionals who would be transforming my look for the shoot. I didn't know what to expect but as the make-up artist worked on my face I saw that her brief was minimal and bare; very different to the make-up heavy, pin-up glamor look I normally favored. After examining me quizzically the hair stylist deemed that my 'Betty bangs' were too short. I didn't even know 'bang extensions' existed until they were deftly being weaved into my hairline.

The wardrobe department was located in a separate room. As a stylist and an assistant began to dress me I discovered that all modesty goes out the window at photography shoots.

'You do know I can dress myself?' I wanted to say as I stood with my arms up in the air like a toddler. The fashion team acted like it was the most normal thing in the world as they squeezed shapewear over my stomach and guided my limbs into leggings and a t-shirt.

These days I don't think twice about standing in my underwear, or often completely naked, as people I barely know manhandle me into clothes.

With my look completed I was ushered out to the main studio, a huge room with high ceilings and every inch painted a bright, sheeny white to maximize the light. It was hard to see where the floor ended and the walls began. There were at least 20 people on set. I know now I was extremely lucky to be starting my career with such a big production shoot and earning a decent fee for it. It took a good two years after the *Heavy* shoot before I even got near to doing that type of job again.

I had realized early on that the goal of the shoot was to make me look frumpy. Trying not to feel self-conscious I followed the creative director's instructions to stand with my bare feet on bathroom scales.

'You need to look sad,' he instructed.

This was my first insight to how models are expected to turn up for shoots as a blank canvas. At the start of my career I had many moments where I struggled with the creative vision of shoots or the fact clients wanted me to look different. There were times when I got upset if I didn't have my hair and make-up done the way I wanted or if I didn't like the clothes. But I learnt pretty fast that it is my job to go with it. You have to be versatile and give people what they want.

There was a flash and a beep from the lighting rig as the photographer began to shoot me from above. At first it was painfully awkward. I was acutely aware of the room full of people staring at me and didn't know how I should pose. I was worried about letting everyone down, but the production team were patient and encouraging. I began to relax listening to the photographer as he darted back and forth shouting out instructions. Now I know that every time the camera shutter clicks you're supposed to do something different. These days, after lots of practice, I have a whole repertoire of 'Tess' poses. I can be playful, somber, sultry or silly on demand and I've nailed the Tyra Banks 'smize' (for those uninitiated with the delicious binge-watching fodder that is *America's Next Top Model* – a 'smize' is smiling with your eyes).

* * *

A month after my photoshoot I was back on set to shoot a TV commercial for *Heavy*. This time the film crew was comprised of a rugged gang of hot, bearded men. They were called 'One Mother Fuckin' Tight Crew' and the testosterone in the room was palpable. Once again I was styled to look drab and my usual rockabilly war paint was replaced with an 'au naturel' look.

I was interested to hear that the make-up artist, who had 30-odd years in the industry, was retiring after the shoot. We got on well and I grilled him for his best stories and tips. In a serendipitous turn of fate, he revealed that a lot of the kit he was using had once belonged to Kevyn Aucoin himself – passed on to him by Kevyn's partner after his death. After telling him how much Kevyn's books had meant to me he gifted me with a kohl eye pencil from my make-up guru! It definitely felt like a full circle moment.

The shoot director was a smoking hot guy with so much charisma I barely registered his missing front tooth.

'Now Tess, do you think you could cry?' he asked as I stood in front of the camera.

Fuck! I hadn't expected that.

For 30 minutes I tried hopelessly to squeeze out a tear, as I uttered my line: 'Losing is my only hope.'

'What music makes you sad?' the director asked.

Five minutes later Damian Rice's 'Cannonball' came floating through the studio. I listened intently and tried to get in the zone. Normally I have no problem shedding a tear. A mere glimpse of a sad animal shelter advert on TV will have me grabbing for the Kleenex. But as much as I tried to shut off my brain I couldn't get away from the fact I was stood in a studio in leggings with a hoard of sexy guys staring at me. It was surreal and acutely embarrassing. Were they really expecting me to pull off a full Meryl Streep? Did they think I was a professional actor? I was barely a professional model! They wanted me to be sad about being fat, but I had worked so hard on my self-image leading up to this point that I couldn't go back to that place.

I tried my hardest to conjure up a mental image of something that would make me cry. Dropped ice cream cones. Abandoned puppies. The death of my beloved pets. Nothing worked.

'How do you feel when people say you are fat?' the hot director tried next.

I gritted my teeth, trying to find some emotion. Nope. Nothing. I just couldn't feel sad about being fat. Not today on this dream shoot. The tears never came on that job and the crew wrapped up with what they'd got.

Afterwards the director took me to meet Miley Cyrus who was filming in a neighboring studio. I had been excited to meet her until she looked me up and down with what I'm pretty sure was a look of disdain.

Tess Holliday's Advice for Life #266:
Sometimes you'll catch celebrities at a bad
moment – they are only human. But some
of them are also just jerks.

Strangely enough the *Heavy* commercial featuring me never aired. They told me it wasn't edited in time but I suspect the real reason was I was crap at crying.

It took me a long time after that to master how to act on film. I think I only really nailed it after I signed with MiLK and Anna Shillinglaw made it her mission to coach me. She made me see that it is my job and I can't goof around. I had to practice a lot to learn how to tap into emotions. Now I can channel things that make me happy or sad – like Miley Cyrus' judgey face.

I was with my Mom when I saw my *Heavy* ad for the first time.

It was December 2010 and Mom was visiting from Laurel. I had taken her to one of my favorite book stores in Pasadena where we were flicking through magazines. I was browsing *People* magazine when I saw it – a full page ad right next to a story about Brad and Angelina! I quickly showed Mom.

'I am so proud of you,' she said, tears filling her eyes.

I snatched up other titles from the shelves flicking though each one. The *Heavy* advert was in multiple national magazines and I bought the lot.

Later that day, a friend texted me: 'I've seen you on a billboard on Sunset Boulevard,' she said.

I screamed, showing the text to Mom and John. Never in my wildest dreams did I imagine my face would be on billboards.

'Can you drive us there to see it?' I asked John.

Normally we'd give the touristy and overcrowded Sunset a hard pass but John reluctantly agreed, driving 40 minutes to get there and parking on the multi-laned street across from the billboard.

'Hey, can we get closer to it?' I asked.

John sighed and put the car into drive.

'Your vanity is getting on my nerves,' he said. He found a closer spot but I was hurt by his reaction. It kind of took the shine off the moment for me.

'I'm proud of you,' he told me later. 'I just think you need to keep some perspective.'

I knew I was not about to give up my nine-to-five, but the buzz surrounding my *Heavy* photoshoot was exciting. Messages began pouring in via Facebook from friends and new fans I'd gained through the Torrid campaign. People from the *Heavy* documentary were adding me on social media.

One afternoon when I logged onto my Twitter account, I saw I had been tagged in a photo J-Lo had tweeted from her balcony at the infamous Chateau Marmont hotel in LA. Behind the photo was my billboard!

A week later I did an interview for *Plus Model Magazine* which sent a whole new audience flooding to my Facebook and Twitter. For the first time I realized how important publicity could be for my career and I was determined to take advantage of every opportunity. Keen to cement 'my brand' I created a Facebook fan page with the updated name 'Tess Munster'. I know, I've had more name changes than Prince, but what can I say? Honestly I probably should have given it a little more thought, but it suited my rockabilly pin-up style at the time.

As 2011 began I was keen to keep the momentum going. I set up a blog called 'My Plus Size Life' and wrote a post detailing my goal to spread the word about 'loving your body at any size.'

'I'm happy you are sharing in my journey, and pleased to meet ya,' I wrote.

I decided I would write about my experiences as a plus-size woman and be as honest and transparent as I could. I didn't know it at the time but I was tapping into something special; an audience that wasn't really being represented.

Joy Nash's 'fat rant' video changed the way I saw myself forever. Despite the pockets of fat acceptance and body positivity online, no one in the fashion world was talking about being past a certain size.

My friend Jes Baker, who blogs as The Militant Baker, is a body-love advocate who has referred to me as the first visibly fat model. A lot of people don't really understand how significant this was.

Over the next few months my profile began to grow. I started to pick up photography jobs through Model Mayhem and my Facebook page. These were mostly low budget shoots where I'd change in the bathroom but at least they were more my own style. I got to wear pencil skirts with polka dots and vintage-style heels and jewelry. Sometimes I'd make $300 or other times I would agree to trade photos for products, posting the shots on my blog and Facebook fan page.

I was still working full time at the dental office so it was hard to juggle everything.

John and his family helped me by watching Rylee whenever they could but I always felt guilty for asking. Especially as I was missing a lot of family functions as I tried to build my career. A fact which did not go unnoticed by his tight knit family.

By now John and I had been together for over two years and I was beginning to wonder whether marriage would ever be on the cards. Not long after we'd met, John had told me he did not want to get married or have children. Perhaps I was naïve, but I always assumed he would come around – especially after seeing the joy Rylee brought to his life. But as my friends started to marry and have children every damn invitation that came in the mail ate away at me, little by little.

Tess Holliday's Advice for Life #267:
Banking on trying to fundamentally change your
partner is shaky ground to build a relationship on.
You're only setting both of you up for heartache.

What hurt me most was that he didn't even seem to value the things I was achieving.

'I thought you wanted to be a special effects make-up artist?' he asked me one day as I told him about my latest modeling assignment. Deep down I knew that his irritation was largely down to the way I had opted out of a lot of family life. Coming from a big Mexican household, family was everything to him. His relatives were his best friends, so he couldn't understand how my upbringing had made me different. I still value family but I've never had a scenario where we do everything together.

I tried to explain why modeling was important to me and how it boosted my confidence. How I had spent a lot of my adult life feeling like an ugly duckling and at last I was being validated. That it gave me a sense of purpose outside of being a mom. But my explanations never seemed to resonate with him.

Whenever I was feeling down I would log on to my blog and write a post about self-esteem and body positivity. I think I largely wrote these to give myself a pep talk but they must have struck a chord with the women reading my blog. I began to receive messages from readers pouring out heartbreaking stories about their lives and the way they had been mistreated. I would always reply doing my best to offer them advice, even though in most cases I was in no position to do so! At a time when I did not believe my partner supported my dreams it felt good to be an inspiration to others. The solidarity from these women who were looking for hope and guidance was addictive, but I couldn't escape the feeling of sadness that while strangers messaged me to tell me I was beautiful, the one person who I wanted to tell me didn't seem to even notice me.

I will admit that I started to withdraw from our relationship and focus on my career. The further away we slipped, the more shoots I booked, the more trips I took and the more excuses I made.

* * *

I was still modeling for small brands earning $500 a time at the most, but by the end of 2011 I had over 100,000 followers on social media – 4 times the population of my Mississippi town. Working at the dental office meant that most of the jobs I did were on the weekend. I didn't want to turn down any opportunity so I would often go to do a shoot or event after work and then stay up writing blog posts late into the night.

One night my vagina practically smacked the laptop out of my hands, and I tried to satiate my need for sexual contact with John. I felt our relationship was floundering physically and I couldn't remember the last time we'd been intimate. His response floored me.

'I'm just not attracted to you anymore,' he said. 'Because of your size.'

For a moment I didn't blink, I thought he was joking. Then I realized he was serious. He wasn't trying to be hurtful, just honest. But it did hurt. I don't expect everyone to find me attractive, we all have things we do or don't like, but for me it's vital for a romantic relationship. The pain hit me like a punch in the stomach. I can take insults from strangers and trolls online but the ones you get from the people you love take a lot longer to get over. As the pain washed over me I thought about Brad and my dad and all the cruel remarks men had made about my body. I was working SO hard to love myself and yet another person I loved had hit me where it hurt the most.

'I do love you,' John said when he saw how upset I was. 'I just don't think there's a spark between us any more.'

His words hung like a cloud over me for days and then weeks. Every time I thought about what he had said I felt that twist of hurt and despair. I felt foolish, ashamed and angry. The way I saw it, true love should be unconditional – not given or taken away subject to a weight requirement.

I agonized over what to do. Should I leave? It was all so ironic. Here I was with a blossoming modeling career, being told I was beautiful and celebrated for my size by everyone apart from the person I loved.

The sad truth was that John and I could not give each other what we needed from a partner. I knew deep down it was the nail in the coffin.

Chapter 11

Eff Your Beauty Standards

Breaking up with John was one of the hardest things I've had to do.

Six months had passed but those unintentionally hurtful words rang in my head as I looked at him sleeping next to me. We were lying next to each other but it felt like we were a million miles apart. I called him my best friend but he felt like a stranger. I realized that I wanted more, I deserved more – and so did John.

I had to accept the cold, hard facts. We had not drifted apart overnight, the problems had been there for a long time. I had pushed them aside but now we had to face them. We loved each other but we weren't right for each other. Our sex life was non-existent and we wanted different things in life.

Although John's words had left me wounded I knew he wasn't the only ass in the relationship. I think it's easy to pass all the blame on to the other person when you have been left hurt and angry after a break up. But if you really want to learn from the experience then you need to be honest with yourself and face up to the things you did. I realized that I had stopped making John a priority and had checked out emotionally months before we were over. When you feel that distant how can you be intimate? Relationships work when you both give it your all and are prepared to hash out the problems. John and I were both guilty of apathy.

Tess Holliday's Advice for Life #273:
Everyone deserves to have a partner who looks
at them the way that I look at a wheel of brie.

When I announced I was moving out he told me he wanted to work at it, but we both knew it was too late for that. So, in March 2012, Rylee and I moved into a one-bedroom apartment a stone's throw from John's home. The rent was $1,000 a month and the apartment complex was so small and packed in that you could hear your neighbours like they were in the same room. The apartment manager Terri, a tiny fireball of a woman with a heart of gold took me under her wing.

My biggest concern was the toll our break up could have on Rylee.

'Will you still be there for him?' I asked John.

'Of course,' he replied with tears in his eyes. 'He's my son!'

Rylee was now five years old and in kindergarten and John promised to do the school run at least a couple of times a week. He would also take Rylee every other weekend – an unofficial arrangement that has remained in place. John is still every bit Rylee's dad, picking him up from school and helping him with his homework. I could not respect him more for the way he cares for Rylee. Despite everything that happened between us, he has always been a good father and loves Ry as his own. Not many men would help pay their ex-girlfriend's rent after breaking up but that's what John did for almost a year. I always knew when things got really tough that John would be there to help us. We are lucky to have him in our lives.

* * *

The aftermath of my break-up with John was a time of self-discovery for me.

When you've been unhappy for a while it eats away at you. If your relationship has been breaking down slowly and steadily it gets to the point where you just feel drained or numb. Like there is nothing left to give. During the last few months of my time with John everything felt heavy. I could still pull off a mega-watt smile or my trademark moody pout at the click of a shutter, but inside I felt completely deflated.

When I am unhappy I can get very negative and as my relationship dwindled I started to see all that was bad in the world. Every little neurosis was amplified and it wore me down. Often I felt overwhelmed with irrational anger and bitchy comments tripped off my tongue. The more I ranted the more it consumed me, making me feel hot and angry and ready to pick a fight with the world. I wrote blogs about loving myself but I wasn't even sure I liked myself. I'd lost my spark and enthusiasm.

I decided it was now time to focus on all the positives in my life; to get out of my head and count my blessings – like the good people in my life. My mom or Heather were always a phone call away and I had recently made friends with Jolene, who at the time was a jewelry designer. She had contacted me via Facebook asking me to model some of her necklaces. When we met up for drinks at Trader Sam's in Disneyland I liked her immediately. We were instantly as thick as thieves and the rest is pretty much history.

Jolene now works for me with the official title 'best-friend-slash-personal assistant' and I'd be lost without her. She is a very patient person who puts up with a lot of my shit and even cares for Bowie on the days I have to work. We are well matched in intensity and she is the first person to call BS on me.

'You're such a laugh liar,' she tells me. 'You always laugh when you're lying.'

We cuss each other out and send each other the meanest messages but we don't argue for long. I always tell her, 'You're the sister I never wanted.'

I've learnt that having positive, like-minded friends around me is essential and I'd urge everyone to find their Jolene. It's important to find the good people in your world. They are the people who are going to help pull you out of whatever messy situation you got yourself into.

* * *

I wasn't sure I'd ever be ready to date again but when a cute Canadian guy messaged me through social media I decided it was a good distraction if nothing else. We went out a couple of times before he invited me back to his hotel and that's where his true motive became clear.

I was just gearing up to get 'back on the horse' so to speak, when my date disappeared out into the hallway. When he returned he was clutching several packets of chocolate and candy. He lay on to the bed next to me like Burt Reynolds in *Cosmopolitan* and opened a packet of M&Ms suggestively.

'Why don't we have sex while I feed you some?' he cooed. Ex-fucking-scuse me?

'I'm sorry but I'm not into that,' I replied as he threw me a look like I'd just stepped on his dog. We didn't go out again and that was my one and only experience of going to bed with a 'feeder'.

Tess Holliday's Advice for Life #275:
Fetishes are totally fine and nothing to be
ashamed of, but you should have a clear
discussion about what you do and don't
consent to before it ever gets to the bedroom.

Being single with a kid meant my evenings were often spent alone. When Rylee was in bed I'd fill the time browsing online or posting on social media. As well as Twitter, Facebook and my blog I also had a Tumblr account and it was there in May 2012 that Nick first messaged me.

At the time I was getting a few dozen messages a day from guys and most of them were along the lines of 'Dam girl u got sum big tits'. Often I deleted the messages without even reading them but for some reason I decided to click on Nick's.

'I love how you inspire other women,' the message said.

When I viewed his profile I was completely stunned. I thought Nick was the sexiest man I had ever seen. When I studied his page further I was amazed by how many similar interests we had. Plus he was funny with perfect grammar and punctuation! I was disappointed when I realised he lived in Australia, but the thought of an accent only added to his allure.

I immediately called up Jolene and told her all about the hot guy who had messaged me.

'You need to get out more,' she said. 'You don't even know this guy and he's in Australia.'

Ignoring her scorn I hit reply and sent him a message. 'Thank you so much, that means a lot,' I wrote. 'And I have to say when I saw your picture I had to pick my jaw up off the floor.'

It took Nick 12 hours to reply during which time I was convinced I'd been too forward.

'Oh God, he probably thinks I am a loser!' I thought.

But despite my blatant come-on we became friends. We talked online most days, swapping details about our lives. Nick worked two jobs, at a boutique store and a coffee shop in Melbourne. He was also an assistant to a music publicist. He was working on getting into a small business program to start a masculine but gender neutral line of accessories and home wares.

When we could work it out in our schedules we began to video chat on Skype. I loved Nick's relaxed Australian drawl and frankly I thought he was hot as fuck. Soon we were talking for hours each day. I would regularly stay up until 3am speaking to him while he navigated his working day. I didn't even care that I had to be up for work at 6am. I could never get enough of him and I still feel the same way.

By now I had a potential job in Australia. A plus-size designer wanted to fly me out and the opportunity seemed perfect. I was all geared up to meet Nick and hoped we would get together. Meanwhile, I joked to anyone who would listen that Nick had 'catfished' me.

Tess Holliday's Advice for Life #279:
Most people are walking around with a cameraphone in their pocket, and practically every laptop is now equipped with a web cam. Even libraries usually have video equipped computers available. If they can't find a single way to video chat with you then BE SUSPICIOUS!

My mom and my friends were concerned he was going to murder me. I got it. Just like them, my advice would be you need to be on your guard, but you have to remember that Nick and I had spent many months talking for hours every day. When you talk to someone on camera every day and hear them interacting with customers, friends, colleagues or even their parents you get to see what they are really like. In many ways Nick and I knew each other better than couples in relationships for years. Being a single mom could be lonely but I always had that warm feeling that Nick had my back. I could talk to him about everything and he would make me feel better. He had a great sense of humor and plenty of sound advice. It was great to have someone to confide in as I navigated the dark side of fame. As each month passed with more modeling jobs and interviews, I was also attracting a growing legion of detractors via social media. I had recently set up an Instagram account, posting photos from my modeling jobs including underwear shots. I would often write about how I was feeling and about my journey to love myself. Once I realized those posts were getting attention and that people responded to them, I wrote them even more. I never really focused on building a following but that's really how it started. I was not deliberately courting controversy but it was clear that many people were not used to seeing photos of someone fat in their underwear. For every ten people who loved me for it, there was someone who loathed it.

The insults were always the same thing: 'you're fat', 'disgusting' or 'promoting obesity'. But my message was that everyone's journey with their body and health should be respected. There is too much pressure on people to look or be a certain way.

> *Tess Holliday's Advice for Life #288:*
> *A photo of a fat person enjoying their life is*
> *no more "promoting obesity" than a photo of*
> *Stevie Wonder is "promoting blindness".*

This was really the time that my love/hate relationship with social media began. Being able to post images and thoughts on Facebook, Twitter and Instagram helped me to build my profile but it had also opened me up to some of the cruelest taunts of my life.

Imagine reading tweets every day that say you are going to die early and it's all your fault that you won't see your kids grow up. In some ways I know it is the price of fame; if you put yourself in the spotlight then you have to expect the scrutiny that goes with it, but that doesn't make it OK. It just made me more determined to call out the everyday insults and judgments that fat people put up with.

The marginalization I felt because of the body I inhabit even extended to my day job, where my colleague had tried to ban me from sitting on the breakroom stools.

'I just got them from Ikea and the weight limit is 280lb,' she said. 'Sorry Ryann, but you can't sit on the stools because you're too heavy.'

Instead she had allocated me an old chair. Of course I immediately plonked my butt on a stool, swiveling around defiantly when she walked in the room. I took a political stand by taking a seat. And no, it didn't break under the strain of my big beautiful butt.

As I was counting down the days to meeting Nick, I was devastated to learn that my modeling job had fallen through. There would be no free ticket to Australia and I couldn't afford to pay for one. My heart was broken.

He had wanted to wait until we met in person to officially say that we were dating, I think in part because of the stigma that meeting someone over the internet still has. But seeing me feeling so helpless and crestfallen he asked me to make our relationship official, and I joyfully accepted.

It's hard to explain how you can fall so deeply for someone you've only spoken to online, but Nick and I had such a deep connection. Then there was the fact he was always complimenting me and telling me he thought I was sexy. He made me feel so comfortable in my skin. I felt completely comfortable to Facetime him in my underwear so he could help me pick out what to wear. Nick still loves dressing me – I'm like his fat Barbie doll.

I was thrilled when I found out that Nathalie Rattner, an extremely talented artist and good friend of mine was heading to Melbourne to be part of a group art show.

'Will you meet up with Nick and tell me what he was like?' I asked.

She came back with a glowing report. 'He's so obviously in love with you,' she said. 'Plus he was impeccably dressed and smelt amazing.'

Of course, now I live with Nick I know that no amount of cologne and grooming can cover up his truly toxic gas emissions.

By now Nick also had put in place a backup plan, working all the hours he could to save enough money to fly over to see me.

'I'm coming in December,' he said. 'My tourist visa gives me 90 days and I want to spend all of them with you.'

We still spent every spare moment talking to each other, but it didn't seem real until he told me the tickets were booked.

On a sunny California winter day in early December, I drove to LAX and walked shakily to arrivals to wait for him. My stomach was in knots. I had gotten changed fifty times, eventually choosing a black-and-white sleeveless dress with a belt and a black satin jacket. As I shuffled nervously from foot to foot I finally spied him. He looked so handsome in a maroon, deep v-neck t-shirt, a tweed blazer and a grey cardigan accessorized with a checked scarf. He smiled as he caught my eye and immediately dropped his bags and walked up and kissed me deeply.

'You're so tiny!' he said, with a grin and his trademark crinkled smiling eyes.

We just stood there for a moment, taking each other in. That's when he realized that he had abandoned his bags half way out of the ramp and was likely about to be tackled by an undercover policeman for being a terrorist. He's still like this, often putting things down and not thinking about it. Australians are far too trusting for America!

We walked to my car and I drove us downtown to a *Botega Louie*, a pretty restaurant on Grand Avenue with high ceilings that is now a regular spot for us. We told our waiter how we had just met in person and he brought us over a complimentary champagne, which was doubly exciting as we were both tight on funds.

That weekend John had Rylee, so back at mine we had the place to ourselves. As soon as Nick kissed me I knew he would be amazing in bed. Our kiss was electric and everything I had feverishly imagined for the last few months. As things got heated I reached up and turned the lights off. After the things John had said my self-esteem had taken a hit, so if I was getting intimate with Nick it had to be in the dark. But Nick got up and turned them back on with a reassuringly gentle smile.

'You're far too beautiful to have sex with the light off,' he said softly.

Any vulnerability I felt soon melted away. I had been told for so long that my body was disgusting but that night Nick made me feel beautiful in a way I had never experienced before.

Now we always keep the lights on and I like being seen during sex. Nick still compliments me every day and I love the story of how we first met. Not everyone would give someone from a different country a chance, fly to meet them and have it work out.

Of course that is just a simplified version of our story. In many ways I am lucky that we survived as a couple at all. I'm ashamed to admit that during Nick's visit I wasn't very fair to him. In hindsight I think in a way I was protecting myself because I knew he was leaving again. I knew I had fallen for him and the loss of control over my emotions terrified me. Despite his doting on me it was hard to trust that Nick liked me too and that we could make this long-distance thing work. Instead I tried my hardest to put up a wall.

My first crime was committed the night of my work Christmas party. I was adamant that I would go alone.

'What am I going to do?' he asked.

'You can sit in my car,' I answered.

So while I was partying with my colleagues poor Nick sat in my car nursing a bottle of orange vodka and watching Stephen Fry on his laptop. I wish I could say that this was the only time I excluded him from my plans on that trip, but that would be a lie.

On Christmas morning I was desperate for Rylee to have some sense of normality. On a whim I decided I was taking him round to John's to open presents. Nick wanted to be included but I didn't want to rub my new relationship in John's face. I left him alone in my apartment for eight hours that Christmas Day, which really is unforgivable. Looking back I wish I had done things very differently.

When we got home it was obvious Nick's feelings were hurt and why wouldn't they be? I gave him the message that I didn't care. The stupid thing is I really did.

For the last two weeks I continued to sabotage the relationship, squandering the precious time we had left by taking extra shifts at MAC. Quite often when I returned home late in the evenings he had cleaned the house and made dinner, after walking around Pasadena where we lived. I think by the time he left he had visited every thrift store within a five mile radius on foot.

Ridiculously, I was removing myself from him because I could not bear that the person I loved was going home to Australia. Instead of cherishing our limited time together I went into panic mode. I think a lot of people behave this way when they are scared to fall in love but they only end up hurting themselves. Opening yourself up for heartbreak will always be scary but sometimes you just have to take the leap.

My efforts to push Nick away were finally thwarted when I got sick with a bad case of the flu. Nick refused to desert me and sent me to bed. He took care of Rylee and walked to the store to get me medicine. Then he nursed me back to health with hot tea and soup. In my feverish state I suddenly had a flash of reality, I was about to lose him if I didn't get it together.

'I'm sorry for being distant and pushing you away,' I finally admitted. 'I know I need to open up more.'

Really it was too little, too late, and I think Nick went home feeling very unsure about our future. We didn't see each other for ten months, and we definitely struggled through a lot of that time.

As we got back to speaking on Skype, Nick encouraged me to open up about my issues. He helped me see that the way I'd acted had come from a place of fear. It's incredibly frustrating at times but Nick often knows me better than I know myself, which helped him understand and forgive my bad behavior. I will always be grateful that he didn't give up on me.

With Nick gone I tried to keep busy. Most evenings I'd attempt to respond to as many emails as I could from fans, mostly asking for advice on getting into modeling. My career was still in its infancy but I offered what I could. I told them to keep on pushing, just like I had done. I also warned them about the social networking site pervs.

Tess Holliday's Advice for Life #290:
Like most things in life there is no secret to becoming a model. Dumb luck plays a big part, but you have to put in the time and effort to be ready to take the opportunity when luck shines on you. Perseverance is key! If there isn't room for you – MAKE room.

When I reflected on my career to date I could see that I needed to enjoy the journey more and relish every achievement. It's not that I hadn't appreciated my opportunities, more that I didn't always stop to take them in. When life is busy it's hard to live in the moment, but now I try to soak up everything. Life is too short so you have to enjoy it.

Bit by bit I was adding money to my 'Australia fund', hoping to make it down under to visit Nick. Selling photos to fans using Paypal was helping a little, but in reality was I nowhere near making enough. As I contemplated selling a kidney, Jolene gave me an idea. I could host a yard sale and clear out my full-to-bursting closet.

So, in April 2013, I gathered up everything I could spare along with my ridiculous collection of hair bows and priced the lot up for sale. Then I advertised it on my blog.

I had an awesome day meeting hordes of fans who were only too happy to take my surplus belongings off my hands. Best of all, I was well on my way to affording my plane ticket.

When I missed Nick, staying upbeat was hard.

One weekend, as I was wasting my time on Tumblr, and Rylee watched cartoons, I came across an awful post.

A bunch of people were having a field day about how disgusting I was and making nasty comments about how I was way too fat to wear stripes or bikinis or show off my arms. Worst of all, a lot of the people agreeing in the comments were fat themselves.

I was really pissed off. Determined to do something I dug out some photos of myself from different modeling shoots. In one I was wearing a bikini, in another a striped dress and lastly in something sleeveless. I cropped them side-by-side and uploaded it to my Instagram.

'If you're tired of people telling you what you should wear, post a picture of yourself with the hashtag #Effyourbeautystandards,' I wrote.

As soon as I posted it people went crazy. Women and men of all shapes and sizes were liking it and posting photos of their own. Within an hour over 1,000 people had shared it and to date my hashtag has been used over 2 million times. Never in my wildest dreams could I have envisaged being part of a revolution. But now women were standing together to say 'enough', and making sure they were not only heard, but SEEN!

That was the day I made it my mission to challenge beauty standards and take on the people and the industries who perpetuate an unrealistic image and I have been outspoken ever since. I am glad to be a positive role model for a group of people who have largely been ignored by the mainstream media. I vowed to continue to live unapologetically and prove my naysayers wrong.

I was soon putting my words into action as I dealt with two men openly ridiculing me during a shoot on Venice Beach.

I had been striking a pose in a blue gingham high-waisted bikini when I noticed the two fitness bros watching from the pier above me. They were pointing and laughing. One pulled out his phone and started taking photos. It was clear they were mocking me.

It was the first time I had been fat-shamed as an adult, aside from on the internet, so at first I was a little stunned. Then I got angry.

'Do you want to go somewhere else?' the photographer asked.

'No,' I told her, standing tall, poking out my tongue and flipping them off. 'Carry on.'

I was determined to keep on posing and not let their jeers stop my shoot. I knew I looked good and there were plenty of people who *would* love these photos. If I ran away now I would be handing them all the power.

It was just another reminder of why I started my #effyourbeautystandards hashtag. I was sick to the back teeth of the intense pressure to conform to my critics or disappear from view. It was my middle finger to a society that taunts and mocks someone just because of the way they look. It was my way of rejecting scrutiny and ridicule and refusing to be held back. And finally it was my call-to-arms to stand shoulder to shoulder with all women that struggle with the same issues.

I was grateful that fame had given me a powerful platform to be fat and proud.

Tess Holliday's Advice for Life #294:
The best way to piss off your detractors is to live well and be happy. It makes them furious.

Chapter 12

The Other F-Word

Standing with my head held high, fat as fuck and as naked as the day I was born, I struck a pose for esteemed photographer David LaChapelle.

As I stood feeling beautiful and strong I thought back to my plump, awkward, teenage self, too embarrassed to be seen in swimwear. But here I was, a US size 22, baring all on a humungous set at Universal Studios, along with around 50 other models. All around me were naked bodies of varying shapes and sizes. It felt sexy and liberating.

When I got an email saying that the legendary LaChapelle wanted to shoot me for a book he was working on I was beyond excited. That is until I read the next line of text, requesting that he wanted me fully nude! I had shot topless in the past but being FULLY NUDE? It was something I had only recently embraced in my personal life and wasn't quite ready to embrace in front of the camera. But when it's an iconic photographer you say yes, no matter how scary it might be. Later that day I talked to Nick about it.

'When people are fat they are robbed of their sexuality,' he reminded me. 'It's important for fat people to show they can be sexy, that their naked bodies can be a thing of beauty too.'

It was exactly the encouragement I needed and I took the job.

Tess Holliday's Advice for Life #301:
Fat people have sex. A lot of it.
And it's really fucking good.

When I arrived at the set it looked absolutely insane. There was a giant dollhouse in the middle and a bunch of naked male models getting sprayed down with Pam cooking spray to give them a sheen. About 100 people were milling around.

I was hungry having just finished work so headed straight to the food table. Bizarrely there was a photo of JonBenét Ramsey surrounded by pizza, chips and gummy bears. I didn't know whether to laugh or cringe.

When I'd finished enjoying the impressive spread, I was introduced to LaChapelle who was lovely and quirky, basically everything I had imagined him to be.

'I adore your look,' he said.

I was relieved to see they had hired some of the best hair and make-up people in the industry – until I heard my brief. LaChappelle wanted the tattoos on my body covered up but my face needed to be bare! I wanted to die. It's easy to be fully nude if you are beautifully made up, but being naked in front of a crowded set with no make-up on seemed like my worst nightmare. I resisted the urge to run away and headed to make-up.

It took two make-up artists at least an hour to work their magic covering up my tattoos. I was grateful when one gave me a wink and discreetly applied some light concealer to my face. Then it was time to go on set and summon the stones to pose proudly in my birthday suit.

Afterwards, I got dressed, said my goodbyes and headed over to production to get my check.

'Hey Tess, thanks for being a part of this today,' LaChapelle said, calling me over.

'Of course,' I replied. 'It was an honor.'

'So Tess, let me ask you,' he said, eyeing me mischievously. 'You're hot. Are you getting fucked regularly? You should be getting it every day.'

We were interrupted by his assistant who handed me my check, at which point I walked out to my car laughing at the ridiculousness of it. Working with a legendary photographer had been amazing and I felt validated as a sexy, size 22 woman. It was liberating.

If I needed any clarification that big was beautiful it was *Vogue Italia* including me in their list of '10 Plus Models Changing Fashion'. It felt like an important step in the right direction, even if I am still waiting for their call for the cover slot!

While Vogue still hasn't come knocking (yet) I did make my Mom as proud as punch by gracing the cover of her favourite magazine *People*, who used me as the face of their 2015 annual body issue. Checking out my groceries and seeing myself looking back at me from the magazine stand was surreal. I still have to pinch myself now.

I had the cover blown up and took it with me to a beauty convention where every other person looked like a Kardashiclone. That day was a blast as everyone complimented my dress, my hair or my make-up. At times I like being the only person who looks like me. People treat me like a unicorn.

I had to laugh at the two old ladies who assumed I had photoshopped my image on to a cover of *People* magazine, because who could believe it was the real thing, right? That cover was later chosen by the American Society of Magazine Editors as a finalist for the tenth anniversary of their best cover awards. Once again it felt great to be breaking away from convention and changing the face of the media industry. As they say on Oscar night 'it's an honor just to be nominated'.

* * *

Often, when people want to criticize me for making waves or stirring up shit (pick one that suits your sensibilities) they hit me with the other F word – feminist. Do they genuinely think that being branded a feminist is an insult? If only they knew that being a feminist means everything to me.

I think, deep down, I was always a feminist, but I had a lot of internalized misogyny until I learnt more about the world around me. Being raised in a religious household, and indeed town, the message was constantly reinforced that, as women, we were there to serve the men who were the head of the household.

But when my father told me I'd never amount to anything I became determined that I would. Now I am the head of the fucking household, alongside my husband. He was raised in a family where his mother was the main source of income – so it doesn't threaten him in the slightest to play a supporting role in my career.

I feel proud to be a feminist every day for a whole multitude of reasons. It could be seeing a woman getting the healthcare she needs because of fellow femmes fighting for her, hearing my son speak about women and their bodies respectfully or living out my dreams just walking around a set full of people, fat as fuck, in sexy lingerie.

Tess Holliday's Advice for Life #312:
You're not too fat to wear sexy skimpy
underwear. Drape yourself in luxurious things,
even if it's just for you – you're a goddess!

When I first got a modeling job with Yours Clothing, a big plus size retailer based in the UK, I was beside myself. I had expected my first international trip to be to Australia but when the company offered to fly me to London they didn't need to ask me twice.

Beforehand people warned me not to have high expectations for London. 'The food is shit and the people are rude,' they claimed.

But I found the opposite to be true. I was infatuated with the straight-talking Brits … and of course the chocolate! (Sorry America, but your chocolate sucks in comparison.) If I could move to England tomorrow I would – straight into a house on Diagon Alley. That is a real place, right?!

On my only day off I skipped all the world-class art and architecture and headed straight to Warner Bros' *Harry Potter* studios in Leavesden to get my Hogwarts fix. I did see some old buildings like Westminster Abbey from the cab window on the way to stuff my face with the finest London pub grub. Priorities!

My *Yours Clothing* shoot was in Peterborough, a city two hours north of London. I had a blast shooting Christmas wear and sexy lingerie and laughed all day. The *Yours Clothing* team were so fun, sending me home with cupcakes and a jar of Cadbury's hot chocolate they had all signed.

Once the shoot was over I travelled to Birmingham for a meet-and-greet at the Bullring– a mall with a huge department store that looks somewhat like a space ship that has just plopped down out of the sky. I was honored to meet fans who had travelled from all across Europe – a girl even made the four-hour trip from Poland! One fan asked me to sign her arm and came back later to show me she'd had my signature turned into a tattoo. I bet she hates me now I call myself Tess Holliday. If you're out there reading this, I'm happy to give you a new signature, and I'll always hold a special place in my heart for the people like you who've been there all along the way.

After a week living the high life I was totally sold on the life of an international model.

* * *

Before I made it to Australia, Nick flew back to stay with me again in LA. This time I had promised to myself to be better and we celebrated our reunion with a little getaway to the Madonna Inn, a resort and spa in San Luis Obispo, California. It was the first time we had spent time away as a couple without Rylee and a much needed opportunity to reconnect. We enjoyed it so much that we stayed for a second night, returning to LA feeling happy and in love.

This time I was determined to be relaxed and fill our time with fun memories. There were visits to Disneyland, nights out at my favorite bars and restaurants and silly movie nights with Rylee. We got little tattoos for each other – I choose a rope heart while Nick opted for a rope knot (although he joked about getting a ball and chain).

A few days before Nick was due to leave I decided to take Nick on a date to my favorite diner in Pasadena. I love it there and always get the chili in a fried tortilla bowl. In hindsight, choosing the most deep-fried item on the menu was probably not the best idea when we had the apartment to ourselves later. I wolfed it down along with chips and salsa before heading home to get romantic.

On the 15-minute drive home I was suddenly aware that my stomach was rumbling. I felt kind of bloated and not one hundred per cent well and by the time we got home I was clenching so hard my butt could have turned coal into diamonds. I ran into the apartment and headed for the bathroom. Before I could help myself I let out a massive fart. I tried to cover it up with a fake coughing fit but when I heard Nick laughing next door I knew he'd heard everything. It was just no good, my ladylike façade was slipping fast.

I started laughing too and then the floodgates opened. The harder I laughed, the harder I pooped, with every guttural noise echoing around the bathroom. I walked out of that bathroom with a look on my face like I'd just returned from war.

'Don't be bummed if we don't have sex later,' Nick said, laughing at my scowling face. But in reality we did, he is no stranger to the human body and is completely at ease with its functions. A refreshing change from the squeamish American men of my past. Now whenever I eat food that probably won't agree with me Nick comments, 'Is this going to be a chili bowl incident?'

'After 'the chili bowl incident' it's a lot harder to embarrass me.

* * *

With Nick back on a plane to Melbourne, I did my best to get back to work.

My profile was continuing to grow and I was getting recognized more every day. Often when I chatted to fans they would tell me how much they admired my confidence and how it had inspired them to show off their own curves.

These women who, like me, had been made to feel embarrassed about their bodies or shamed by strangers were fighting back. They were emboldened by my message and ready to love themselves. In less than six months my #EffYourBeautyStandards hashtag had been shared 400,000 times on social media. It was amazing.

Whenever I had the opportunity I would attend 'body positive' events, often with other plus women. I'd show off my figure and reinforce my message that every body is beautiful. Soon I had an army of new plus friends: cool, inspiring women all doing their bit to change beauty standards through social media and blogs.

Over the years I have been on Amber Rose's 'SlutWalk', stood in my bra and jeans at peak hour in Toronto's Union Station to promote body diversity, and taken part in all kinds of other protests and events calling for an end to racism, sexism, fat-shaming, transphobia or any other kind of bigotry. For me, just existing in public is an act of feminism and body positivity, because when I wear something that is deemed 'inappropriate' for my body type people always stare.

Tess Holliday's Advice for Life #319:
When people stare, hold your head high and
know that you are giving a middle finger to society
and challenging the way people view beauty.

Fired up by the knowledge that my message was reson-
ating with people, it got me thinking about what else I
could do to empower women.

As 2014 began, I knew my 'brand' was a strong one
and friends kept telling me I should do more to capital-
ize on it. I had observed the way some unscrupulous
celebrities had made millions promoting anything and
everything on social media but it didn't really sit right
with me. If I was going to make money from the brand I
had built for myself I wanted that venture to be authentic
and meaningful.

When a photographer friend approached me with
an idea I knew instantly that it was the thing I had been
looking for. A sound business idea that would inspire my
fans and make them feel beautiful was born – a pin-up tour.

The idea was to create 'pin-up for a day' packages,
inviting fans to come to a photography studio and get
their hair and make-up done. I would help style them in
beautiful corsets that we had available for the shoot and
show them how to pose. The end result would be gorgeous
professional photographs as a keepsake of the day.

I hoped it would prove popular but when I announced
it on social media the response was insane. We got over

1,000 emails in an hour. The first shoot was supposed to be just a day in Texas but it soon turned into three days due to the demand. I was also being inundated with requests to bring our pin-up tour to basically every city in the country.

The Texas shoot went like a dream. It was amazing to meet my fans who would bring me gifts and cry when I hugged them. Their excitement was infectious and I loved meeting all kinds of women from different backgrounds. I have so many memories from the tour but one of my favorite moments was seeing a sassy African American lady strut on set in a black corset with thigh high boots.

'Are y'all ready for big nasty?' she triumphantly declared as she slid down on the floor to strike a seductive pose. I instantly feel in love with her style and attitude.

The first tour was such a success and the requests continued to roll in so we began to expand to other places adding a different location to the schedule every month. Our crew would fly to a city on Friday, spend Saturday shooting and come home on Sunday. We still could not meet the demand so we extended to two dates a month.

I still had a full-time job so it was hard work traveling at the weekends. For 12 hours a day I was in full 'Tess Munster' mode, returning to LA depleted and exhausted only to get up for work at 6am the next morning. The only thing that kept me going were the wonderful women we met. Eventually something had to give.

In February 2014, I made the decision to quit my job and be a full-time model.

It was terrifying giving up a steady 9 to 5, especially as I had a child to support but sometimes you have to be brave and take a leap of faith. The pin-up tour had empowered me and given me the financial security to leave.

With my schedule freed up we travelled all over. I loved having more time for Rylee and then spending the weekends he was with John meeting my fans.

It was amazing the way the pin-up shoots brought people out of their shells. Some women were over fifty and had not had photos taken since their high school senior photo. There were also lots of accountants and schoolteachers who wanted to feel sexy. They would turn up with wild shoot concepts and give it their all. I guess the old joke rings true, the more buttoned up you are at work, the crazier you are underneath, because it seemed the meekest women were the ones who when put in front of a lens wanted to set loins on fire! I loved it when they asked to shoot topless or with a riding crop or fetish wear. Nothing felt better than hearing women say the experience had changed their lives.

Tess Holliday's Advice for Life #323:
Every woman deserves to feel in charge
of and empowered by her sexuality.

Because of Mom's ordeal during my childhood, raising awareness of domestic violence had been a cause close to my heart. In April 2014 I had another idea that I was sure could really take off. People were always asking me when I would make merchandise, so I thought I would start by selling t-shirts with #Effyourbeautystandards emblazoned on them and donate a portion to the National Coalition Against Domestic Violence. My intentions were pure, but it turned into one of the biggest mistakes of my career and severely damaged my reputation in the process.

From the moment I advertised my venture on social media the orders began flooding in. Jolene and I were attempting to deal with the orders ourselves but soon we were in over our heads. We were determined to find a supplier that was ethical and had the same product from size small to size 4X (the largest we could find). We didn't want someone to order a small and an extra-large and have the product quality be different. Fat people are often made to feel like an afterthought in fashion, and we didn't want anyone to feel like that. Unfortunately the only supplier who offered what we needed was in hindsight ridiculously expensive.

We didn't realize it until people started complaining, but the sight we were using had failed to account for orders properly. Somehow about 140 fans were not sent t-shirts. Suddenly it was turning into a massive clusterfuck with people calling for blood online and posting blogs about how I was a shitty person who set out to intentionally scam people.'

After trying to fix the issues myself for far too long, I hired a distribution center to take over. Sadly the damage had already been done. As I sent out the last of the replacement t-shirts, issued refunds and paid all the people involved it was clear I was operating at a loss. I felt embarrassed and guilty. I donated $1,000 to the charity out of my own pocket, which when supporting both my son and mother on my own on a $15 an hour salary was frankly more than I could afford at the time. I hoped it would make up for my mistakes but it only fueled my online critics.

'You must have made $20,000,' one speculated. 'It's not enough.'

Others created a narrative that I used the money to go to Disneyland, despite the fact that we had season passes that only cost us $30 a month, our one indulgence.

The criticism kept on coming and eventually I did an interview with *Bustle* explaining what had happened and apologizing to my fans.

I was so mortified by how it all turned out that I've been reluctant to sell merchandise ever since. If I do try again I know now to hire a professional company to oversee it and make sure I have a foolproof plan in place. I know some of my fans are still angry with me about it but I have definitely learnt from my mistakes.

* * *

The pin-up tour continued for 18 months. Every date we posted sold out with people jetting in from far-flung corners of the country and the globe to strike a seductive pose with us. I loved seeing how complete strangers at shoots would support each other and even trade clothes they'd brought along. Friendships were definitely made on that tour.

I met so many amazing women but the one who sticks in my mind the most was a lady whose husband had died in a car accident the week before the shoot. He had encouraged her to take part so she wanted to take nice photos to honor him. It was hard for her to be composed in front of the camera but she was amazing and pushed through. We were all crying with her.

Afterwards she told me how lucky I was to have Nick. 'Make sure you have all your affairs in order,' she said. 'Hold on to your relationship and cherish it.'

I stayed in touch with her after the shoot and I often think about her heartfelt words.

Six months had passed since I'd last seen Nick but in June 2014 I finally made it out to Australia to visit him for his 30th birthday. Rylee was spending a month of his summer holidays in Laurel with Mom and my grandparents, a tradition we have continued ever since. It's a welcome break for Ry who enjoys going back to his roots, exploring my grandparents' woodland and chasing fireflies. I'm glad he loves it as it's important to me that he has a close bond with my family in the South. I know he'll cherish those times as he looks back.

Knowing Rylee was in safe hands, I loved exploring Melbourne, a beautiful, cosmopolitan city with winding cobblestone laneways where tiny cafés and bars seem to appear out of nowhere. Nick was so proud to show me his home, taking me to all his favorite haunts and proudly introducing me to his circle of friends.

The day after I arrived was International Women's Day and touchingly Nick's best friend Tamara had invited me to speak to young female students at the school where she taught. I was guest of honor at a special breakfast with around 100 mothers and their daughters, aged 13 to 17, in the room. It was nerve-racking!

I had no experience of public speaking but did my best to speak from the heart, opening up about my mom being shot, how I was bullied at school and why I made the decision to drop out. I explained how, despite everything, I know that education is important and that you should never give up on your goals.

'I was always told I could not accomplish my dreams because of my size,' I explained. 'But you can be whatever you want to be. Do not listen to the critics.'

The audience gave me a standing ovation and their kindness and enthusiasm was completely humbling.

With my fan base in Australia slowly building, I was thrilled to be able to host meet-and-greet sessions in both Melbourne and Brisbane. In Melbourne I could barely hold back the tears as a lady in her thirties shared her experience of losing her son.

'When I looked through my photographs I realized I only have a few of us together,' she told me sadly. 'I was much more comfortable behind the camera because I hated the way I looked.'

I knew this was a sad reality for many moms who struggle with their bodies post-partum. I could recall visiting the beach with Rylee as a toddler and dodging photographs in my swimsuit.

'From now on I'm going to care less,' the woman told me. 'I want to embrace my memories, that's what's important.'

Tess Holliday's Advice for Life #326:
Don't let how you feel about your body rob
you from making memories with the people you
love. You might not feel good about yourself in the
moment but you will look back and be glad that
you have a record of those cherished moments.

In Brisbane, the city where Nick grew up, I was amazed to meet fans who had flown across the country and waited six hours in line in the blistering heat just to meet me. I can only apologize to the people I hugged for being a sweaty, hot mess. What can I say? Even winter days in 'Brisvegas' can be brutally hot!

I also met Nick's parents Rosemary and Geoff (or Ro and Beautiful Geoffrey as they are affectionately known) in this gross, stinky state.

'Show 'em your shots,' Nick said, handing them a pile of sexy prints I had ready to autograph.

'I love them!' Nick's mom Ro declared, as she studied a photo of me in nothing but skimpy lacy underwear, my prodigious white booty barely covered. At first I was embarrassed but she was completely genuine. Like many Australians, Nick's parents are as laidback as they come.

After eight hours of meet-and-greets on my feet in the Queensland heat (Dr Seuss eat your heart out) I was very ready for a lie down. And I did, except it was on the tattoo table. I had long admired the tattoo artist Mimsy, who is famous for working out of a retro trailer in Brisbane. She is a creative genius with a beautiful whimsical style and I wanted her to craft a scene of mermaids and seahorses with a rainbow-colored clam shell on my right thigh. Incredibly Mimsy completed it in four and a half hours, which is insanely fast for such an intricate tattoo. I mean, my thigh is a pretty big canvas! We are lucky to now call her and her family close friends.

As I stumbled out feeling a little light-headed, Nick rushed me back to his parents to eat and rest. I always tell people that getting a tattoo is a test of endurance, so like a marathon you need to eat a high protein meal and drink a lot of water on the day you have it done. I also avoid caffeine and take ibuprofen beforehand. Good tattoo artists will give you a break if you ask or take a break themselves, giving you a chance to stretch and relax.

I had always wanted my legs heavily tattooed and I was so ecstatic with the finished result. As soon as the skin under my coral paradise had healed I donned a pair of denim short shorts that I had been saving for the occasion. If I wasn't a model I would probably have my legs completely covered, but not every client likes tattoos so I am holding back – for now at least. (But I have to admit my will power is weakening!)

Four days before I was due to fly back to LA, Nick treated me to a surprise evening out in Melbourne for my twenty-ninth birthday.

He took me to get my nails done, and let me know that he had secretly hired someone we had worked with on a recent shoot to meet me back at the hotel for hair and make-up. He told me he just wanted me to feel good for my birthday.

'You look beautiful,' he said kissing me. 'Let's stop by a photo booth on our way to the restaurant.'

Throughout our relationship taking silly snaps in photo booths had kind of become our thing. I've always loved the classic vintage ones. The type that flash so brightly you get spots across your eyes and print sticky, grainy, rotten-egg smelling shots in black and white.

Arriving at the chemical photo booth, Nick and I squeezed inside. I sat on his lap as he put the coins in and preened myself ready to strike a pose. As the camera flashed Nick pulled a gorgeous 1940s diamond ring from his pocket. My heart stopped for a second. He winked and asked me to marry him. I cried, he cried, and it's all caught on film. The photos are so perfect people often ask if it was staged.

I flew home to LA a few short days later feeling like the girl who had it all. I was going to marry the man of my dreams. 😏

The five months before we saw each other again felt like the longest of my life. I kept busy, continuing the pin-up tour and drowning my sorrows during nights out with Jolene. Being a 9pm pajamas kind of girl, I thought my party days were over but Jolene insisted on taking me out.

'You need to have fun,' she told me.

So we'd go out drinking and head back to hers to stuff our faces with nachos and donuts. She'd yell at me for getting crumbs in her bed and then I'd pass out and take up all the room. Despite all that she is still my friend. Our hashtag is #goodtimesbaddecisions.

That Christmas, hopelessly lovesick, I flew back to Australia with Rylee in tow. This time we stayed in Brisbane housesitting for a friend of Nick's family and largely avoided going outside. Queensland summers are humid and insanely hot (even worse than Mississippi) so we went to the movies a million times that trip. I think we saw every kid's film twice.

I also returned to Mimsy's pink trailer to get a pineapple girl tattoo on my right inner calf. It's not every day that someone tells you they want a tattoo of a pineapple girl who looks like a California raisin but of course Mimsy nailed it.

* * *

In January 2015, back in the USA, I woke up to pandemonium. There were at least a hundred text messages on my phone and my social media was going crazy. I was making headlines all over the world.

A couple of months before, prior to leaving for Australia, I had agreed to sign to a boutique model agency in London called MiLK. I'd received an email from the agency's founder and managing director, Anna Shillinglaw, that had immediately sparked my interest: 'I know you are unconventional but you have a great face and are great with the camera,' she said. 'I'm interested in signing you.'

Anna, a striking brunette in her early forties, had a lot of success as a model in the 1990s. I liked that she was no nonsense, honest and blunt, which is quite an English thing. She didn't promise me the world but said she would work hard to take my career to the next level.

I signed with her soon after she got in touch but agreed to do a test shoot before we announced it officially. We agreed that seeing as I was getting married I would ditch the 'Munster' and rebrand as Tess Holliday.

That January morning, MiLK had sent out a press release detailing how I had made history as the first model of my size to sign to a major agency. The story had gone crazy. It was all over the press and I was getting dozens of requests for an interview.

Tess Holliday's Advice for Life #333:
I DID IT! THIS FAT GIRL DID IT! And you
can also do anything you want to. Don't let your
or anyone else's preconceived notions about
what you can and can't do hold you back.

Anna organized everything and set up some amazing publicity. Within a week I had been interviewed on *Today* and was a guest on *The Meredith Vieira Show* in New York. I also did interviews with *Cosmopolitan* and the *Daily Telegraph* in London, plus tons of online publications.

As my name went mainstream I gained thousands of new social media followers but I also became a target for online trolls. Suddenly the cyberbullying soared to a whole new level: *She signed with MILK management. How convenient. MOOOOO … Love your body? … yeah do it a favor and stop shoving cake into it … The only ground she's breaking is the one she treads on.*

It was hard to see people saying stuff like that but there was no way they were raining on my parade this time. I tweeted: 'Never read the comments.'

Then I agreed to do an interview with *Huffington Post* about the outcry.

'I get that not everyone understands what I am about but to me it is such a simple concept,' I told the interviewer. 'It's all about loving your body regardless of your size and chasing your dreams.'

I've realized that while bullying never goes away (it just takes on different, more sophisticated forms) it doesn't have to define you or ruin your life. Awful, vile things are said to me on a daily basis and this bullying isn't just from 'kids', it is from adults who should know better. Pressing the notifications buttons on social media is always a minefield.

Every week I get messages that tell me: *You're too fat, you're going to die ... you look like a whale ... I bet no one ever has sex with you, you're a bad parent ... you're going to kill your kid ... you're promoting obesity ... you're a bad example for women ... I bet your baby is drinking straight fat when you feed him ...*

It used to make me really mad but now I just think, 'Fuck you! I don't care.'

Some people are idiots. The only way they would be happy is if I crawled on to a cross and crucified myself.

Sorry assholes, that's not about to happen.

Tess Holliday's Advice for Life #336:
When you embrace the things that people
see as your flaws, you rob them of any
power their words have to hurt you.

Chapter 13

It's a (Mostly) Wonderful Life

As I started to get used to the frenzy over my career I was grateful to have Nick by my side. Whether he was encouraging me to be brave or traveling around with me to shoots, life was always better with him in it.

By now my excitement for long-distance travel was rapidly wearing off as I spent half my life on airplanes.

When Nick returned to the USA in April 2015 we travelled all over for shoots and interviews, once again living in each other's pockets. It was fun when we got to fly business class – but also grueling. Traveling for hours on end and then heading straight to shoots was tiring. At times I would be so busy I'd forget to eat and end up feeling faint. Nick would run to my aid, dashing off to find snacks and plying me with protein bars and sips of coca cola.

When jetlag struck I wasn't always on my A game and during one bikini shoot in London I almost had a breakdown. Ironically the theme of the shoot was being kind to yourself, but that photoshoot was very difficult for me. The bikinis didn't provide a lot of support and I was worried everything would fall out. On top of that I disliked my hair and make-up. Before long I was crying in the fitting room and Anna had to rush over to the studio to talk me into it.

'Tess, I know this is hard but you need to figure it out,' she told me bluntly. 'This is your job.'

Although I didn't much like it at the time I knew she was right. Modeling isn't always easy but no one wants a diva on set. Now I know that you have to trust that everyone there wants you to look good. They've got your best interests in mind so you have to go with it.

* * *

As Nick's stay came to an end I began to feel sad. There was no way I want him to leave.

We had planned a vacation in Las Vegas to celebrate my thirtieth birthday with a few of our close friends and family, and we decided together to throw caution to the wind and get hitched there.

Up until now, our plan had been to organize a big wedding at Mom's place in Mississippi and invite all our friends and family. But I loved the idea of tying the knot on my birthday, especially as it was exactly a year since we'd got engaged. We could do it rock 'n' roll style, at a Vegas chapel.

We chose the Little Church of the West, a gorgeous cedar-clad chapel that looks like it's straight off the set of a Western. It is where Elvis Presley and Ann-Margret exchanged vows in the film *Viva Las Vegas* and celebrities such as Judy Garland, Zsa Zsa Gabor and Cindy Crawford got married there.

'We'll still have our wedding in Mississippi,' I reassured Mom, who had promised to care for Rylee in Laurel, giving us the freedom to head off to elope.

We spread the word quickly among our close-knit friends. We were thrilled when 15 friends, including Nick's brother Andy and his girlfriend Nicole, said they intended to make the trip.

Our whirlwind wedding outfits were created by Barrie Kaufman, a Western-wear designer friend, whose clothes have great attention to detail. She whipped up an Elvis-inspired blue jumpsuit with gold-fringe for Nick and a teal blue cowgirl outfit accessorized with little gold stars for me. She'd never created menswear before and Nicks first outfit gave him more camel toe than a Sheiks stable, but with a few tweaks we were both in love with the look. How she pulled it off in such a short amount of time I will never know.

Our friend Joe Dirt walked me down the aisle. He is a true original – and showed up wearing an old tux jacket with the sleeves cut off and no shirt. The ceremony was short, sweet and full of laughter. Nick wore vintage yellow shades, which was just as well as he bawled like a baby. Our friends cheered as we were pronounced man and wife.

We continued the celebration at Dive Bar, which is owned by our friend Angie, where we toasted our nuptials with whiskey and ate meatball sliders and pizza. Nick and I were so happy, not even caring when Joe almost set the bar on fire with sparklers. We danced the night away to *King vs Cash*, a vegas band with two lead singers who take turns on the mic, one singing Elvis covers, the other Johnny Cash. What else do you need?

We returned to my tiny abode in LA as newlyweds, relieved that this time Nick was coming home for good. Before long Rylee returned, making three, then Mom moved in and we were to up to four – three more people than we had bedrooms.

After divorcing Bill, Mom had married again only for her third marriage to hit the skids. It was just too painful for her to continue living in Mississippi so she moved to LA for a fresh start. I loved having her around but it was kind of a ridiculous set up.

Nick and I slept in the dining room, with a folding screen our only privacy. Mom and Rylee shared a room with their beds separated by a partition. There were rumors on the internet that I was worth three million and there we were, four of us living in a tiny 800-feet, one-bedroomed apartment. It was like Charlie's house in *Willy Wonka and the Chocolate Factory* – my mom's favorite movie – with us all crammed in and tripping over each other.

In normal circumstances I would have been making enough money for somewhere bigger, but until Nick's

Green Card and 'right to work' authorization came through I had three members of my family to support.

I was not the only one feeling the strain. Leaving his family, friends and support system behind in Australia was a big challenge for Nick. He had moved to a new city, 8,000-odd miles from home, to live in a shoebox with his new wife, an emotional mother-in-law and a moody ten-year-old. Everyone needs space, but for Nick, who has suffered from chronic depression related to Bipolar disorder for most of his life, it was so much harder.

When Nick first told me he had depression I thought, 'Yeah I get it, I get sad too.'

However, I soon discovered that I had no real grasp of the struggles he's been through.

Nick has always endeavored to talk openly about having clinical depression, social anxiety and borderline personality disorder. He's been hospitalized for it and is keen to fight the stigma attached to mental illness. Really, it is his story to tell, but what I can say as his partner is that our relationship and life as a family often hinges on his moods.

Anyone who's spent a moment with Nick will tell you how charismatic, smart and funny he is. When you talk to him he makes you feel like you're the most interesting person in the world, and the only one in the room. But there is also a deep well of sadness in him, and until you live with someone it's hard to really know the true extent of their demons. Now I know that some days can be unbearable for him. When he is struggling even the simplest tasks such as calling to pay a phone bill can be daunting. It means that during those times I end up doing a lot for him. I try to be patient and I take a lot of things off his plate that I know cause him emotional stress. He is very self-aware, reads a lot and wants to get better, but it's a mental disease.

When our lives are stressful with constant travel and strict deadlines I know that is not the best environment for Nick. I try to be conscious of how what I do or say can affect him and do my best to communicate clearly with him – an ongoing battle for someone used to retreating and hiding from my feelings.

Nick is on medication which helps with the highs and lows but it's still tough. It's affected me more than I would probably like to admit and at times I don't understand why he gets the way he does, but that's OK. When he gets angry and volatile and can't cope with his feelings all I can do is support him. He is always quick to apologize and try to explain what led him to that point.

We try to keep our disagreements out of Rylee's earshot but if he does witness an argument we talk to him afterwards. It isn't always easy but he understands. He is a very loving and compassionate kid. Living with someone with clinical depression has been a rough learning curve. I've realized that if I want my marriage to work I have to accept Nick's flaws in the same way he has had to accept mine. You can't change your partner, you have to take them as they are and find a positive way to deal with the challenges. When Nick is in a bad place I remind myself that it is temporary and eventually he will feel better. I also talk to my therapist and I'm part of an online support group for partners with BPD.

Our marriage hasn't always been easy but we make it work. We may fight like cats and dogs, but we have so much passion for each other, and that's never gonna change. It has made us think carefully about how we post online because sometimes it feels like a lie. When people say, 'You guys are the perfect couple!' or comment '#RelationshipGoals' on our Instagram posts they have no idea what may be going on in our home. But when all is said and done we support each other, even if we are fighting.

Tess Holliday's Advice for Life #341:
When someone you love hurts you,
hate the behavior, not the person.

In mid-October 2015, we added two rambunctious rescue cats to our tiny one-bedroomed home. We were already stressed from the cramped quarters and my instincts told me something was off with my body. Uh oh. I peed on a stick and confirmed my suspicions – I was pregnant. My first instinct was to panic. Nick was having a tough time adjusting to life in LA and would often say he wasn't sure about having kids. How would he handle this?

Three more frantic pregnancy tests and a trip to Planned Parenthood later there was no running away from the truth. It felt like I was 19 all over again.

As inner turmoil consumed me I agreed to appear on a Russian TV show. Google translate tells me the Russian phrase for 'shit show' is Шоу дерьма; feel free to correct me if that's wrong, potty mouths of Russia.

The presenter kicked it off by asking me if I ate hamburgers all day and then to really spice things up he invited the audience to ask me questions, which it seems was just an elaborate way to insult me.

'You are a role model to my wife but I would like her to lose weight,' one man said. 'Most men want to give their women chocolates or roses, but when I look at you all I want to give you is a workout video.'

'It sounds like the only thing your wife needs to lose is you,' I replied, trying to keep my voice calm.

The next person to take the microphone suggested I was too fat to ever get pregnant. Oh the irony. I desperately wanted to correct him but I was worried that it might get back to Nick before I had a chance to break the news myself.

The excruciating interview done, I left the studio, quietly simmering with fury. I was amazed, not for the first time, by people's audacity to pass judgment on someone's health at a mere glance. None of us can just look at a human being and know their health issues, the food they eat or how active they are.

Am I fat? Yep. Am I lazy? Nope. I know I take my health seriously. Why should I list what I eat or how often I work out to justify my body shape? That's nobody's business but mine.

Tess Holliday's Advice for Life #345:
You can't tell anything about someone's
health by looking at them.

Tess Holliday's Advice for Life #352:
You don't have to justify your health status to
anyone. All bodies are valid regardless of what
issues you might be facing, whether they are genetic
or a result of how you've lived your life. Bodily
autonomy is fundamental to human rights. Your
body is your business and yours alone.

I didn't know how to tell Nick about my pregnancy. I was terrified of how he would react. I should have known he would be shocked but supportive, but childhood experiences had my negative thoughts on overdrive. What if he flipped out? What if left me and went back to Australia? The thought petrified me. Whenever we went out and Nick handed me a drink I would pretend to take a sip or spit it back out. Then at home I'd dump wine in the sink when he went to the bathroom. Luckily he's an Australian (read: drunkard) so is more than happy to finish my drinks for me.

One morning over coffee with our friends Roxx and Cats they brought up having children. They talked about their plans to use IVF and a donor, being a same sex couple.

'Do you want to have another kid?' Roxx asked us.

'I guess I'm just so apprehensive because of my genetics, I don't want to pass on my mental illness to a child,' Nick replied. His answer left me fighting back tears but I didn't let on. They reassured him that he was in the best possible position to guide and nurture a child with mental illness, but unbeknownst to him the damage from his response had already been done.

Really, it's amazing he did not notice I was pregnant as I felt like I could puke 24 hours a day. I could not stomach anything greasy and I was off my carbs, which should be a giant red flag! All I wanted to eat was fresh fruit and nuts.

For some crazy reason I confided in no one, not Jolene or Anna, my agent. Not even my Mom. I carried on working long days modeling, flying around the world. How I avoided vomiting on my stylist-provided shoes I will never know... there were a few close calls!

I wish I had a cute story about how, at three months pregnant, I eventually told Nick but the truth actually came out during a heinous fight.

That night we were all going to dinner at Outback Steakhouse (my mom and I shamelessly love it!) and somehow I had got myself into a massive mood about what Rylee should wear. Most of the time Rylee likes to dress like an old man but that night I wanted him to wear a shirt I had picked out. But Nick let Rylee wear what he wanted and I was pissed. When Nick jumped in the shower I made Rylee change. Then when he returned I threw my husband a smug look.

'What do you think you are achieving?' he asked. 'You have to pick your battles with him!'

It erupted into a screaming match until Nick stormed out the apartment to go for a walk around the block and cool off. When he came back he started packing.

'What are you doing?' I demanded.

'I need to think, I'm going to a hotel,' he replied.

'No, you're not,' I fumed. Then, as he tried to leave, I blocked the doorway.

'Please get out of my way,' he said wearily.

'Please don't go,' I said, digging into my bag for the letter confirming I was pregnant to thrust it at him.

'You're pregnant?' he said, his eyes filling with tears. 'Why didn't you tell me?'

'I was scared,' I replied.

'How far along are you?' he asked.

'Twelve weeks.'

The revelation left him stunned and we talked a lot about what we should do. Some people might frown on the fact that I was married, three months gone, but still considering the options, but I had to be sure the decision to have a baby was right for both of us. I don't think there is anything wrong with that.

Having raised one son alone after a teenage pregnancy no one knows more than me the sacrifices and commitment that bringing up a child entails. Anyone who dismisses the real challenges, blindly thinking love conquers all, is doing themselves a real disservice.

Two nights later, during a night out, Nick turned to face me. He was buzzed on Jameson but had a big smile across his face and tears in his eyes.

'We're having this baby aren't we?' he said.

'Yes!' I replied ecstatically.

I touched my stomach protectively, at last excited about the new life inside me.

With the decision made to have our baby, we broke the news to Rylee and Mom with a surprise Christmas Day reveal. As we were giving out gifts, I handed Mom and Rylee a small package. Inside was a music box and, lifting the lid, Rylee found my 15-week ultrasound. On it I had written 'Baby Holliday is on the way'.

'Ry,' Mom cried. 'You're going to be a big brother!'

'Yeah, but not right now!' Rylee said, looking confused.

'Right now!' Mom said. 'That's a sonogram of the baby in your mamma's belly! She's pregnant!'

Over the next week Rylee had lots of questions.

'How are babies made?' he asked. 'How did Bowie get here?'

While we didn't share that his impending sibling was the result of one too many spicy watermelon margaritas and a deliciously dirty romp at The Standard hotel, we were honest with him.

After a quick rundown of the birds and bees I explained that Nick and I cared about each other and had made the decision to have a child.

'What happened when I was born?' he asked next.

'Your father did not want to be involved,' I told him gently. 'It's OK if you feel sad about that and you can ask me whatever you want.'

I know that Nick and I have a different approach to parenting compared to my other friends who have kids. I grew up too sheltered so in many ways I do the opposite. Rylee may be young but he already knows that everyone has a right to choose what to do with their body. That might seem extreme but I think it is important for kids to know. In my opinion body autonomy is the last thing you should give up. If you've lost that right, what do you have left?

Knowing that Rylee might be feeling insecure about the latest addition to the family I decided to get a tattoo especially for him. We drove to San Diego to see our dear friend Jackie Dunn Smith, a talented painter and tattoo artist, to render a little kid in a bear costume on my foot. Rylee's bear 'baby' has been his constant companion throughout his childhood. He's often guarded with his emotions, but when he saw the tattoo a grin spread across his face from ear to ear. I love that tattoo and every scrap of love it represents. Once I stop breastfeeding I will get one for Bowie too.

In the past I would blindly trust tattoo artists but as I got older, and arguably wiser, it has been important to me to research the artists and make sure they are good.

Tess Holliday's Advice for Life #355:
A tattoo shop should always be pristine – it's like a minor medical procedure. If a place doesn't look clean or professional then get the fuck out of dodge. There are enough tattoo studios around. At the very least the artist should have gloves on and use fresh, sterilized instruments that are opened from their protective packaging in front of you. Don't be afraid to ask to see their sterilizing equipment if you feel unsure.

As my bump grew we kept the secret within the family, eventually announcing our news in February 2016.

With Anna managing me I continued to be busy, working and traveling until I physically couldn't any longer. It was just after we'd gone public that the paparazzi began to follow me. The first I knew of it was when I saw an article in the *Daily Mail* with all kinds of shots of me going about my day. It was kind of creepy seeing photos of myself as I filled my car with gas and headed to a hair salon. They even had shots of me clutching a parking ticket I'd found on my window. I feel fairly confident it's the most glamorous photo of a person getting a ticket ever taken!

To add insult to injury, people in the comments section were criticizing me for wearing a traditional Mexican dress.

'But I didn't know I was being photographed!' I thought. 'This was my down time.'

Nick said he was mad too – but for altogether different reasons. That day he was wearing a flowing wool camel cloak, a large vintage hat and carrying his ukulele in a tweed case. He felt like Stevie Nicks but got cropped out the picture. The struggle is real!

Joking aside, that day was the beginning of the end of my privacy and now I get papped all the time in LA. They even stalk me within the walls of Disneyland with my kids. Some days it feels horrible and invasive but I've come to accept it as part of the job.

Most weeks people stop me wherever I go and I've even had a fan waiting for me outside my toilet cubicle … I would not be where I am now without my fans so I'll do whatever I can to be accommodating. Unless one of my kids is sick or needs me, I will really never refuse a photo. Occasionally I'll ask someone to wait when I am working. People often don't understand that I am not being dismissive, it is about doing my job. Just like everyone I have obligations and need to be professional at work.

I share so much of my life publicly that it's hard when people want more and more. I think women can often mistake Nick's gregariousness and support for women as an invitation to behave in a way that can make me uncomfortable. It can be tough, but then there are the fans who are so incredibly supportive. They come to everything I do and even send me gifts for my kids. When I get lovely letters from them their support means the world to me. I know I have supporters who would defend me to the bitter end and I am very lucky.

Tess Holliday's Advice for Life #362:
If you are reading this book, thank you for
your support. I would be lost without you
guys! My success is your success too.

The hardest thing about being pregnant this time round was going through it publicly and everyone offering me advice or passing judgment. People invade your life and believe they know everything about you. I lost count of the tweets saying I was too fat to have a healthy baby or asking me to prove my health. The constant tweets of Twitter twats helped me understand why so many celebrities fall off the radar for a year when they have a baby. Pregnancy hormones and online bullying are not a good mix. My doctor had told me that my numbers were perfect but sometimes it got too much for me. There were plenty of moments where I cried.

One charming fucker took time out of her day to shoot and edit a video about how I am an awful person who would kill my child, which honestly says more about her than it does about me.

At the time I was seeing a personal trainer three times a week but why should I divulge that just because someone is fat-shaming me? In truth I made peace with exercise when I made the decision to take the pressure off myself. If I don't want to go to the gym, I won't. Instead I'll take my kids to Disneyland and walk a half dozen miles while enjoying the park. Believe it or not, this fat girl does get her cardio – but not at the demand of trolls. You can say what you like, but I'll do it my way.

'Every time I looked at my tummy, it is a reminder of how amazing my body is,' I wrote on Instagram. 'Even though I've had a baby before, I didn't love myself entirely … So now every kick, every pain, is incredible to me. I get constantly shamed and criticized for existing in this body, but the problem isn't my size, it's others inability to comprehend that beauty doesn't come pre-packaged in one size. I'm embracing my stomach getting bigger, stretch marks and loving this little life I'm growing.'

I was seven months pregnant when I decided to kick my defiance up a notch by posing naked with my back to the camera for the *Telegraph*. Predictably my critics had a field day but it left me feeling empowered – a final 'fuck you' before my baby arrived.

* * *

Just like Rylee, Bowie was delivered by scheduled Cesarean section at 40 weeks, arriving into our world on 6 June.

I had looked into a VBAC (vaginal birth after Cesarean), but after talking it through with my doctor I took his advice to have a Cesarean. The hospital staff were great apart from the pre-op nurse who, I shit you not, asked me SIX times if I had diabetes.

'Fat people can have a healthy pregnancy,' I eventually told her. 'So no, I do NOT have diabetes – just like the last five times you asked.'

All my irritations were swiftly forgotten as an hour later Bowie Juniper Holliday came crying into the world, a healthy 8lb 10oz baby boy. We had chosen the name as a tribute to the late, great David – an inspiration of Nick's for his complex masculinity.

'It would be great for him to have a name that is gender neutral,' Nick had reasoned. 'It will allow him to be whatever he wants to be.'

Seeing Nick hold our little starman for the first time was incredible. He looked so stunned and happy and I will always cherish that memory. We laughed and cried and wondered what the fuck we had gotten ourselves into. I finally knew was it was like to have a baby with someone I love. I will never forget how full my heart felt.

After five blissful but sore days in hospital we took Bowie home. By now we had a new house in LA with four bedrooms to fit our growing brood. Rylee, Bowie and my mother all have their own rooms. It's surreal that we now can afford to have so much extra room … although it's STILL not enough room for all of my clothes. I often look around our home and think we would not be here if I hadn't taken those often terrifying steps to follow my dreams.

I was concerned about healing well but frankly I spent more time worrying about everyone else. As soon as I got home I felt pulled in all directions. Checking emails for work, making sure Rylee was adjusting to having a new brother and trying to make sure that Nick was doing OK too. He did as much as humanly possible to help, but as a breastfeeding mother who struggled to pump milk a lot of the early responsibility fell to me.

Having a baby for the second time I knew what to expect and as my hormones shifted I could feel the familiar feelings of post-partum depression creeping back. I had experienced being a mom to a newborn, but ten years is a long time between babies and not only had I forgotten a lot, a lot has changed. I was often plagued with insecurity as I obsessed over doing everything right for Bowie. I was second-guessing myself every step of the way when really I should have chilled the fuck out.

Thankfully I had my friend Jen, who writes the Plus Size Mommy Memoirs blog, on speed dial. She was my Yoda and connected me with experts on lactation, baby wearing and anything else I could need until I started to feel competent again.

Being a new dad was challenging for Nick too. When Bowie was born it changed our dynamic. We went from a long-distance relationship, to living together, to having a parent living with us, to having a baby all at break-neck speed. Caring for a newborn and coping with the constant crying and lack of sleep was a big adjustment. I would be lying if I said having a baby didn't put a strain on our relationship. But I don't think there are many new parents out there who haven't experienced this to some extent. It made us stronger than ever.

When Nick is struggling mentally he needs a lot of attention and when I'm busy with Bowie I can't always give it to him. I see him recede into himself and I don't always know how to deal with it. And then there's the joy of working through all this in the public eye, which adds another layer of pressure.

Nick always says that Bowie is the best thing he has ever done. His eyes sparkle when he is around him and they are already mischievous best friends. Having Bowie has totally changed him and I know, even when it's tough, he wouldn't change it for a second.

I went back to work just five weeks after giving birth, spending hours in make up to shoot my first clothing line MBLM by Tess Holliday. It was being launched by Penningtons in Canada and we'd spent the previous eight months in design meetings and working on fabrics and prints.

My collection included clothing that was sheer and figure-hugging, with studs, grommets and bold prints – things that are often missing from the boring plus size apparel on offer. I often had to fight to make the hemlines higher and the necklines lower.

It's hard for any new mom to go back to work so it was a relief to be able to take Bowie with me for that shoot and the many more that came after it. The Penningtons' team flew to me so I didn't have to travel far and could nurse Bowie, which was a massive weight off my mind. I am pretty sure the stylists loved having a baby spit up on me as they tried to work. Who wouldn't?!

Designing and then modeling my own clothes has been a dream come true for me. I would love to continue to push edgy alternatives to the same old garbage on most plus size hangers. I have always had my heart set on producing a diverse lingerie line – I want to cater for girls who have tummies and small boobs and every other body type that miraculously isn't a 'perfect' hourglass shape.

Tess Holliday's Advice for Life #367:
There are as many body variations as there
are stars in the sky. Every body type
is beautiful and worthy of love.

While hair and make-up teams could effortlessly transform me from mom to glam, feeling sexy did not come easily after I had Bowie. As I looked in the mirror, six months after having a baby, I barely recognized myself. My stomach had got lower, my breasts were a different shape and I had a galaxy of fine new stretch marks. I went from feeling in control and in love with myself to feeling like a stranger in my own body.

After the brutality of birth and intensity of breast-feeding this should not have been a shock. Even for me, a woman who had been on an intense journey to self-love, it really was. I decided the time had come to be honest with my fans. Posting an intimate photo of my belly to Instagram, I opened up about my battle to learn to love my body post-partum.

'I think it's important to be honest about what it's like to be a woman in the media who recently had a baby,' I wrote. 'I was fat before, I carried a healthy baby, and guess what, still fat … and THAT'S OKAY. I have no New Year's resolution to lose weight, but only to work on learning my new body and loving and nurturing it.'

I signed off urging anyone struggling with body issues to find the strength to be their own cheerleaders. The post was met with an amazing response with hundreds of women and men agreeing to my sentiments. It was very empowering and the pick-up I needed. At times like this I find social media powerful and wonderful. I would be lost without it – a reality that I had to face when Facebook suspended my account.

I had shared screen grabs of comments from a troll, but I couldn't understand why I was the one being punished – why Facebook shut down MY page. When no one from the company would respond to me I decided to tweet about it.

It wasn't the first time Facebook had wrongfully removed my content. While I was pregnant with Bowie they had removed photos of me in a bikini claiming that it violated health standards! The photos were allowed back on the page but I had to wonder. Was someone at Facebook fat-phobic?

As soon as I went public my account was quickly reinstated but the situation left me fuming. 'Would this be happening to me if I wasn't plus sized?' I wondered.

As I continued to take baby steps back to loving myself post-pregnancy, I decided to step out my comfort zone and do something brave. I would walk a runway in skimpy underwear, belly wobbles and all. I've been very vocal about how Victoria's Secret should cater for plus sizes so I loved Buzzfeed's idea to set up a Victoria's Secret style fashion show doing just that. Instead of tiny Miranda Kerr and co, our models would be different sizes, shapes and gender identities.

It was really a final frontier for me to wear low-waisted panties that showed off my belly but I did it with Nick's encouragement. Afterwards I was on such a high. Facing up to my insecurities about my body felt so freeing. What are you waiting for? Give it a go!

Since then I have regularly shared post-pregnancy photos of my body using my hashtag #Effyourbeautystandards.

I've also talked about the pressure of having to do your day job when your baby has kept you up all night and all you want to do is cry.

'This is the reality of being a mom,' I wrote, sharing a snap of my red, puffy, exhausted face after two hours crying.

At the end of the day, life isn't a contest to show how much you have or why you think you are better than everyone. I prefer to be authentic. Sharing my journey in this way makes me feel less alone. I hope it makes some of my followers feel less alone too. I want them to know that it's OK to speak up about the difficulties of being a parent. I feel so many women out there try and fool everyone into thinking their life is perfect, but shit gets real and it's OK to admit you find it tough. I do think honesty is the best policy – even if it lands you slap bang into the middle of an angry political debate …

When I decided to wear a 'Dump Trump' t-shirt for a photo during the election season I was amazed to lose around 200,000 followers. And then, to add insult to injury, those assholes voted him in. Go figure.

When shit like that happens it makes you not want to be outspoken and I do sometimes wonder if I am making life harder for myself. Being politically engaged is just part of who I am. I'll fight for what I believe in, even if it causes controversy. You can bet my fat ass on that.

Tess Holliday's Advice for Life #370:
A society should be judged on how it treats
its worst off, not how it treats its best off.

Epilogue

So what is life like as the first successful, visibly fat model?

A while back Rylee caught me moping on the couch.

'Mom, are you sad about being fat?' he asked. 'Because being fat is kind of the reason you're famous.'

I hugged him and laughed, thinking, 'Wow, he's right, how the hell did I get here?'

In truth, I often wonder how I went from an unhappy, fat teenager to a plus size supermodel. (Every time I say 'supermodel' I can't help but sing in my head Jill Sobule's song 'Supermodel' – Cher Horowitz eat your heart out!) How did it become my calling to contribute to a new movement to treat all bodies with the love and respect they deserve?

I think part of the reason I was so adamant I wanted to model was that growing up I had no one to aspire to who looked like me, other than Miss Piggy and Roseanne (Sidenote: If either of you comes across this somehow – lets be BFFs.). Later in life Beth Ditto would set my fat little heart on fire, but I spent so many of my younger years feeling like a freak who should apologize just for existing. I loved fashion and make-up and wanted to express myself, but where were the famous fat models to look up to for inspiration? There were women out there with larger bodies, and I am fortunate enough to now call many of those trailblazers friends – but no one was really FAT. I am glad to be part of a movement that has changed that.

When I started out on this journey I was still working out who I was and coming into my own. I was guarded but now I know I am more of myself, the real me, and that's important. It's not my job to make everyone like me. It's important to show people that you can do whatever you want to do and size shouldn't hold me back. Some people will like it and other people won't.

When I look back at my achievements I am honored to be a model in a world that doesn't celebrate bodies that look like mine. There are so many highlights from my career to date but I feel proud that I made history by signing with MiLK and had moments, like appearing on the cover of *People*, that challenged beauty standards.

Of course, fame has come at a price with teenage bullying now replaced by trolls online. If I had known what I know now — how I would be singled out, condemned and ridiculed — would I still have done it? These days I even get criticism that I don't 'represent' plus bodies when I am literally the ONLY visibly FAT plus size, mainstream model. I will also fight with everything I have to make sure that I help open the door for more women of color, more trans models, and a wider representation of ages and sizes. I may not look like you, but I'm fighting to make sure someone who DOES makes their way into the public eye.

Living my life under the constant scrutiny of strangers never stops being hard. There was a time when I could freely post photos of myself, food, my sons, just my life, without being attacked. But now everyone thinks that they know me and I am judged for every move I make. People want my job, my friends and even my husband. The boundaries get crossed often.

Everyone has their vices but mine are visible. If I have been shooting for eight hours straight then yes, I want a chocolate croissant.

I'm often asked, 'Since you are a role model, why not promote healthy living?' But size is not an indicator of health and it's not my place to tell women they need to lose weight or what to do with their bodies. Your body, your business. You don't have to justify or prove your health status or owe an apology to anyone. Do I believe in taking care of your body the way you see fit? Absolutely. But I also believe the diet industry is a multi-billion dollar business trying to sell unobtainable body standards. It counts on the fact that millions of women (and men) will feel shitty about themselves and buy their products in hopes of unlocking some secret to fill the hole that those feelings create.

The fact that I'm plus size, wear crop tops and love to have a cupcake now and then, is not dooming our young women into a life of misery. If anything, it should show others that you can enjoy your life the way you want to.

Imagine what would happen if we all started to love ourselves a little bit more and worried less about what others thought? What would that look like? My message is about loving yourself in your current form. Life is so much more beautiful and complex than a number on a scale.

I've realized that it doesn't matter what I do or say there's always someone who is not happy. I have to do what makes me happy and feels right in my gut. Fuck everyone else. Have I made mistakes along the way? Yes, but that's part of being human.

There are days when I get up in the morning and feel amazing about myself, but there are also days when I feel lousy. An online jerk could say something that is false or irrelevant to my life, but sometimes it still hits a nerve.

It's also an odd feeling to have women writing to me, telling me how much I have changed their lives, or inspired them, when behind closed doors I might be feeling like a hot mess. It's at times like this that I turn to the good people around me, I reach out and accept help and support – and importantly I remember to believe in myself. At the end of the day, being in a magazine isn't what makes me happy, it's having people around who absorb and reflect my confidence. A high tide lifts all boats – as women we need to raise each other up as much possible.

* * *

I started #effyourbeautystandards out of frustration. I was tired of being told I was too fat to wear a bikini, show off my arms or whatever other ridiculous restrictions people place on plus size women. What I didn't know at the time was it isn't just a plus size problem, it's not gendered, it's something we all deal with.

Women are still viewed as sexual objects instead of equals, they are disregarded, and disrespected and then labeled 'angry' or 'volatile' when they stand up and oppose this treatment. Something needs to give. It's not a radical idea that women deserve the same opportunities, that we don't exist for male consumption and that our bodies are ours to do with what we want, but we are still fighting for these things. If the world is going to improve we need more voices from all sides of the equation. We need to hear from people existing in all bodies – a spectrum of size, gender, sexual orientation, religion, skin color, race, and disabilities. We need protests, legislation to protect us, and lawmakers to take us seriously. We need to keep speaking out against injustices.

Being a feminist means I try to change how women are treated and viewed around the world and to stand up for those that can't – and that is why everyone should be one, regardless of your gender orientation. Some people think that men can't be feminists but I'm definitely married to one. And as for my sons? They are one hundred per cent being raised as feminists.

Ultimately, #Effyourbeautystandards is not about being fat or saying 'eff you' to thin and healthy people, it is about loving your body no matter what gender, size, height or color it is. It doesn't matter if you are fat, ugly, thin, healthy, love to eat cheeseburgers or love to chomp on carrots; you are deserving of love and happiness and you have the right to live your life as you please without scrutiny. Aim high with your dreams and goals. Be who you want to be, eat what you want to eat, strive for what you want and don't apologize for it. If it's your route to feeling happy then that's good with me.

* * *

When I was a single mom in Mississippi I wondered if I would be on my own for the rest of my adult life. But eventually some stupid Australian came along and decided he wanted to woo me. Friends used to tell me I was silly to hold out for true love, hinting that as a 'fat girl' I should not be so picky. Well, guess what, refusing to settle worked for me. Rest assured, if I can find someone to love my FAT ass, then everyone can.

I've come to realize that a lot of people will never take me seriously. I'm still too fat and too short and not up to their beauty standard but hey, that's OK. As long as I'm giving life my best and loving the skin I'm in, I'm on the right path.

As a kid I was obsessed with Disney and wanted a fairytale ending. After all the horrible things I endured it felt good to escape into a fantasy world and dream big.

I know now I wasn't meant to live a fairytale life, I am supposed to live MY life. The one where I keep pushing for body positivity and equality, the one where I do not hide my curves, the one where I stand tall as a formidable fat feminist.

Every day I feel honored to be able to inspire people with my work and words. Knowing I have some impact on others is what keeps me going. If there is someone out there I can help or who needs to hear it, then fuck it, I'll carry on.

My Thank You Page

Thank you to my best friend, and the person that gives me sweet sweet lovin', my husbear Nick. None of this would have been possible without your love, snack plates, support, back rubs, and for showing me that I deserve to be loved in the body I exist in. I hope to be by your side for a long time, or until the whiskey kills you. Thank you to my boys Rylee and Bowie for making me a better person and for giving me a reason to keep going. I hope I've made you two proud. Thank you to my mom for constantly driving me bananas and reminding me that I could achieve the impossible. I did it Momma! (And I guess it wasn't a phase, I'm still weird!) Thank you to my Maw and Paw for stepping in when we needed help the most; I love you both so much and take full responsibility for the grey hairs! Thank you to my Grandma Hoven for always making me laugh when life wasn't easy & for making the effort when others didn't. Thank you to Heather, Steve & Rose for loving me when I didn't even quite know how to love myself. Thank you for believing in me and never giving up, even when I tested you all.

Thank you to Jolene (and Liz) for being my ride or dies, the sisters I never wanted, and for teaching me how to finally have fun! Now let's go party until 6am – strip mall massages on me! Thank you to Tracy/Mama D for believing in me and using a fat model when no one else was; I will never forget what you did for me. Thank you to John for being a father to Rylee, for supporting me on this crazy path (even if you didn't always agree with it) and giving me tough love when I needed it. Thank you to my OG LA girls and my other soul sisters: Doreen for being my sounding board, introducing me to my love of burritos, and for feeding my funfetti addiction, and to Cindy for always being there for me and Rylee – you always keep it 100! Thank you to my agent Anna for doing the impossible and helping to make my dreams a reality, and for all your hard work. Thank you to Charlotte and Kelly for guiding me through the crazy process that made this book a reality.

Thank you to my "glam team" Tony, Jorge & Meaghan for making my ridiculous big hair, never enough highlighter & lingerie as outerwear dreams a reality! Thank you to my Eff Your Beauty Standards team: Rainbow, Natalie, Kelvin, Ali, Aarti, and Katie: you guys have helped me make my dream of spreading body positivity and self-love to the world and I will never be able to repay you. Thank you to everyone I've met along the way, those who believed in me, my followers who supported my dreams no matter how ridiculous. I couldn't have done this without you. Thank you to Little Debbie for your delicious snacks that made my childhood bearable, and honorable mentions to boiled peanuts, cheese, peanut butter, dark chocolate, and gummy bears – you're the real MVPs! Last but not least, thank you to Ice T who once told me 'haters hate up!' and he was right. To my haters, you know who you are, and thanks for the motivation!

About the Author

A UK size 26 and US size 22, Tess Holliday is the largest supermodel to be signed by a major modelling agency, Milk Management, and has fast become a global phenomenon. Tess is credited with really shaking up the fashion industry, forcing it to question the norm, and spearheading the body positive movement with her #EffYourBeautyStandards campaign.

A hugely popular social media star, she has more than 1.5m followers on Instagram and 1.7m on Facebook from around the world, especially the UK and Europe, US, Canada, ANZ and Mexico.

Tess attracts a lot of press attention – she was a cover star for PEOPLE Magazine and makes regular appearances on *Mail Online*, *The Telegraph*, Buzzfeed, *The Guardian*, *Independent*, *Marie Claire*, *Glamour* and *Cosmopolitan*.

She was voted one of the top six plus-size models in the world by *Vogue Italia* and made *TIME* magazine's 30 Most Influential People on the Internet.

Loud, proud and very funny, Tess's humorous yet emotive take on life as a modern woman will follow the trail blazed by Bryony Gordon, Caitlin Moran, Amy Poehler and Tina Fey with her distinctive voice.

Tess is married and lives in LA with her husband and two children.